VALUES AT WAR

Selected Tanner Lectures on the Nuclear Crisis

VALUES AT WAR

Selected Tanner Lectures
on the Nuclear Crisis

Freeman Dyson

Raymond Aron

Joan Robinson

Sterling M. McMurrin, *Editor*

UNIVERSITY OF UTAH PRESS   Salt Lake City   1983

LIBRARY OF CONGRESS CATALOGING IN PUBLICATION DATA

Dyson, Freeman J.
Values at war.

"Selected from The Tanner lectures on human
values" — Introd.
Includes bibliographical references and index.
1. Atomic warfare — Moral and ethical aspects —
Addresses, essays, lectures. 2. War and literature —
Addresses, essays, lectures. 3. Atomic weapons and
disarmament — Addresses, essays, lectures. 4. Arms
race — Economic aspects — Addresses, essays, lectures.
I. Aron, Raymond, 1905–   . II. Robinson, Joan,
1903–   . III. McMurrin, Sterling M. IV. Tanner
lectures on human values. V. Title.
U263.D95   1983   172'.42   83-21705
ISBN 0-87480-226-1

CONTENTS

The Tanner Lectures on Human Values

THE TRUSTEES

THE ADVISORY COMMISSION

DEREK C. BOK
President of Harvard University

DONALD KENNEDY
President of Stanford University

HAROLD T. SHAPIRO
President of the University of Michigan

INTRODUCTION

The crucial problem of our time is the very real possibility of nuclear war with its total destruction. The essays in this volume, by scholars of the highest competence in the analysis of contemporary affairs, treat this problem from various standpoints — military, political, economic, biological, psychological, social, and moral — indeed from virtually every possible point of view. Their primary interest is not in describing the consequences of nuclear war, which they regard as a final holocaust, but in identifying the possible causes of war and exploring the possibilities of its prevention. A central concern of each of the authors is the competition in nuclear armaments — how to stop it and turn the world around toward the immediate reduction and eventual elimination of nuclear weapons.

In his unusual essay "Bombs and Poetry," Freeman Dyson, British-born mathematical physicist at the Institute for Advanced Study in Princeton, defends the thesis that "cultural patterns are more durable than either the technology of weapons or the political arrangements in which weapons have become embedded." Dyson's analysis of human attitudes relating to the instruments of war, from the guns of World War I to tactical nuclear weapons, and his intimate knowledge of the scientific, engineering, and political history of nuclear weapons give his statement special value. But it is his optimism of hope, despite the present threat of world suicide, that gives his essay its distinctive character. "Hope," he quotes from his friend Clara Park, "is not the lucky gift of circumstance or disposition, but a virtue like faith and love, to be practiced whether or not we find it easy or even natural, because it is necessary to our survival as human beings."

The celebrated philosopher of history and politics Raymond Aron of the Sorbonne and the Collège de France, in "Arms Control and Peace Research," provides the reader with a historical analysis of the basic issues engaging the United States, the Soviet Union, and Europe in their confrontation on armament control. He treats the relation of revolution and war to political and economic systems, pointing out that "ethnic rivalries and historical conflicts survive revolutions and remain equally alive even when governments profess the same ideology."

A distinctive feature of Aron's essay is his statement on the work of "peace research institutes" in their studies of the causes of war and the conditions for peace, whose work on the whole he has found disappointing. They have not found the real causes of war and have failed to adequately define a ground for peace. Aron's analysis of the political attempts to establish an effective arms control in relation to both military policy and technological progress is especially valuable for those concerned with the current debates on such matters as the MX and international arms negotiations.

In her essay "The Arms Race," Cambridge University economist Joan Robinson recounts the decisions and actions that brought the world to the edge of destruction and describes the international economic and military complicity, inordinate nationalistic aspiration, and failure in political morality that obstruct the achievement of grounds for peace.

These essays were selected from *The Tanner Lectures on Human Values* (published by University of Utah Press and Cambridge University Press, England). The Tanner Lectures, which are endowed by the American scholar and philanthropist Obert C. Tanner, are delivered annually at Clare Hall, Cambridge University and Brasenose College, Oxford University in England and at Harvard University, Stanford University, the University of Michigan, and the University of Utah in the United States.

STERLING M. McMURRIN
Editor

Bombs and Poetry

FREEMAN DYSON

THE TANNER LECTURES ON HUMAN VALUES

Delivered at
Brasenose College, Oxford University

May 5, 12, and 19, 1982

FREEMAN DYSON was born in England and educated at the universities of Cambridge and Birmingham. During World War II he worked as a civilian scientist at the headquarters of the Royal Air Force Bomber Command. After the war he went to Cornell University and became Professor of Physics there. Since 1953 he has been Professor at the Institute for Advanced Study in Princeton. His professional work has been mostly on technical problems of mathematical physics, but he has written a number of articles on broader issues for a wider public. His autobiography, *Disturbing the Universe*, was published in 1979. He is now writing a book on war and weapons which will be an expanded version of these Tanner Lectures.

INTRODUCTION

I chose the title "Bombs and Poetry" for this series of lectures, because I want to discuss the gravest problem now facing mankind, the problem of nuclear weapons, from a literary rather than a technical point of view. Poetry means more than versification. It means the whole range of human reactions to war and weapons as expressed in literature. The main theme of the lectures will be the interconnectedness of the bombs and the poetry. I will be exploring the historical and cultural context out of which nuclear weapons arose, and at the same time looking for practical ways of dealing with the problem of nuclear weapons in the future. My hope is that an understanding of the cultural context may actually help us to find practical solutions. Basic to my approach is a belief that human cultural patterns are more durable than either the technology of weapons or the political arrangements in which weapons have become embedded.

The three lectures are independent of each other. You may come to any one or two of them without feeling obliged to come to the others. The first lecture, "Fighting for Freedom with the Technologies of Death," is a historical account of our involvement with weapons since 1914, giving special attention to the tactical nuclear weapons which now constitute the most immediate threat to our survival. The second lecture, "The Quest for Concept," examines various alternative doctrines or policies which have grown up around nuclear weapons, and tries to define a doctrine which may offer us some long-range hope of escape from the trap into which reliance on nuclear weapons has brought us. The third lecture, "Tragedy and Comedy in Modern Dress," places the problem of nuclear weapons into a wider context, as the contemporary manifestation of a human predicament which is as old as the Iliad *and the* Odyssey, *the doom of Achilles and the survival of Odysseus. Each of the three lectures is arranged like an old-fashioned sermon, with historical examples at the beginning and a moral at the end.*

*   *   *

I. FIGHTING FOR FREEDOM WITH THE TECHNOLOGIES OF DEATH

The title of today's talk is borrowed from a recent book written by Steve Heims and published by the M.I.T. Press, *John Von Neumann and Norbert Wiener: From Mathematics to the Technologies of Life and Death.* I will be talking about warfare and technology from a historical point of view. I shall be trying to answer two questions. Why has war always been so damnably attractive? And what can be done about it?

In the impressions of World War I which I absorbed as a child, technology was a malevolent monster broken loose from human control. This view of technology was then widespread, not only among poets and literary intellectuals but also among scientists. The most memorable description of the war which I read as a scientifically-inclined teenager came from the biologist J. B. S. Haldane:

> A glimpse of a forgotten battle of 1915. It has a curious suggestion of a rather bad cinema film. Through a blur of dust and fumes there appear, quite suddenly, great black and yellow masses of smoke which seem to be tearing up the surface of the earth and disintegrating the works of man with an almost visible hatred. These form the chief parts of the picture, but somewhere in the middle distance one can see a few irrelevant-looking human figures, and soon there are fewer. It is hard to believe that these are the protagonists in the battle. One would rather choose those huge substantive oily black masses which are so much more conspicuous, and suppose that the men are in reality their servants, and playing an inglorious, subordinate and fatal part in the combat. It is possible, after all, that this view is correct.

Haldane published this vignette in 1924 in a little book with the title *Daedalus, or Science and the Future,* which I found in the school science library at Winchester. It sold well and was widely read in scientific circles. Haldane had been an outstandingly brave and conscientious soldier. His friends in the trenches had given him the nickname Bombo because of his attachment to a noisy experimental trench-mortar which he liked to carry around in the front lines and blast off unexpectedly from time to time. His cold and clinical view of the battles of 1915 extended also to the future: "The prospect of the next world-war has at least this satisfactory element. In the late war the most rabid nationalists were to be found well behind the front line. In the next war no-one will be behind the front line. It will be brought home to all concerned that war is a very dirty business."

The soldiers of all nationalities carried home from World War I memories of pain, death, and physical squalor. The lasting image of war was men sharing a mud-filled ditch with corpse-fed rats. The degradation of the living left in men's minds a deeper revulsion than the sacrifice of the dead. During the years leading up to the outbreak of World War II, when my school-friends and I looked ahead to the future, we were not sure whether being killed would be worse than surviving. Wilfred Owen's poem "Mental Cases," in which Owen is describing survivors of the battles of 1917, gave us a picture of what might await us if we were unlucky enough to survive:

> Who are these? Why sit they here in twilight?
> — These are men whose minds the Dead have ravished.
> Memory fingers in their hair of murders,
> Multitudinous murders they once witnessed.
> Wading sloughs of flesh these helpless wander,
> Treading blood from lungs that had loved laughter.
> Always they must see these things and hear them,
> Batter of guns and shatter of flying muscles,
> Carnage incomparable, and human squander,
> Rucked too thick for these men's extrication.

Most of us did, unexpectedly, survive. And then, only a few years later, the invention and use of nuclear weapons carried the technology of death a giant step further. The nuclear bombs with their mushroom clouds make Haldane's vision of war, the black explosions attended by doomed and puny human servants, look even more plausible. How could this have happened? How could supposedly sane people, with the stink of the trenches still fresh in their memory, bring themselves to create a new technology of death a thousand times more powerful than the guns of World War I? To answer these questions, I look again at the career of Robert Oppenheimer. Oppenheimer is a good example to illustrate how it happens that people get hooked on weaponry. A rich new source of historical facts has recently become available, throwing a fresh light on Oppenheimer and on the mental climate out of which nuclear weapons grew.

The new source is the volume of *Letters and Recollections* of Robert Oppenheimer edited by Alice Smith and Charles Weiner.* It gives us a far more authentic and many-sided picture of Oppenheimer's personality than we had before. In January 1981 I met Robert's brother Frank at a meeting in Toronto and thanked him for allowing Smith and Weiner to publish Robert's letters to him, which are in many ways the best and the most revealing in the whole collection. "Yes," said Frank. "At one time I had thought of publishing his letters to me in a separate book. But it is much better to have the five or six characters Robert showed to his various friends all together in one place."

In 1932, when Robert was twenty-seven and Frank was nineteen, Robert wrote a letter to Frank on the subject of discipline. "But because I believe that the reward of discipline is greater than its immediate objective, I would not have you think that discipline without objective is possible: in its nature discipline involves the subjection of the soul to some perhaps minor end; and that end

* Cambridge: Harvard University Press, 1980.

must be real, if the discipline is not to be factitious. Therefore,"
he concluded, "I think that all things which evoke discipline:
study, and our duties to men and to the commonwealth, war, and
personal hardship, and even the need for subsistence, ought to be
greeted by us with profound gratitude; for only through them can
we attain to the least detachment; and only so can we know
peace." I have pulled these sentences out of their context. It is
true, as Frank said, that Robert's letters to him show only one face
of a six-faced mountain. But still I believe that these two sentences
contain a key to the central core of Robert's nature, to the sudden
transformation which changed him eleven years later from bohe-
mian professor to driving force of the bomb project at Los Alamos.
Perhaps they also contain a key to the dilemmas we face today in
trying to deal wisely with the problems of nuclear weapons and
nuclear war.

How could it have happened that a sensitive and intelligent
young man in the year 1932 put war on his short list of things
for which we should be profoundly grateful? This little word
"war" appears in his letter untouched by any trace of irony.
Oppenheimer's gratitude for it is as sincere as the gratitude of
the poet Rupert Brooke, who greeted the international catastrophe
of 1914 with the famous words: "Now God be thanked who has
matched us with His Hour." But Brooke died in 1915, and his
reputation as a poet was irretrievably smashed in the years of
muddy slaughter which followed. The poets whose works survived
the war and were read by the literary intellectuals of Oppenheimer's generation were the poets of plain-speaking disillusion-
ment such as Wilfred Owen. It comes as a shock to find Oppenheimer in 1932 writing about war in the manner of Rupert Brooke.

There were of course other voices in the 1920's than Haldane
and Owen. I do not know whether Oppenheimer read *The Seven
Pillars of Wisdom* by T. E. Lawrence, a man whose many-sided
strengths and weaknesses curiously paralleled his own. Lawrence
was, like Oppenheimer, a scholar who came to greatness through

war, a charismatic leader, and a gifted writer who was accused
with some justice of occasional untruthfulness. *The Seven Pillars*
is a marvelously vivid and subtly romanticized history of the Arab
revolt against Turkish rule, a revolt which Lawrence orchestrated
with an extraordinary mixture of diplomacy, showmanship, and
military skill. It begins with a dedicatory poem, with words which
perhaps tell us something about the force that drove Robert
Oppenheimer to be the man he became in Los Alamos:

> I loved you, so I drew these tides of men into my hands,
>   And wrote my will across the sky in stars
> To earn you Freedom, the seven pillared worthy house,
>   That your eyes might be shining for me
>   When we came.

And with words which tell of the bitterness which came to him
afterwards:

> Men prayed that I set our work, the inviolate house,
>   As a memory of you.
> But for fit monument I shattered it, unfinished: and now
> The little things creep out to patch themselves hovels
>   In the marred shadow
>   Of your gift.

And there was Joe Dallet. Dallet was the first husband of
Robert Oppenheimer's wife Kitty. Born into a wealthy family, he
rebelled against his background, became a Communist, and organized a steelworkers' union in Pennsylvania. In 1937 he went to
Spain to fight on the losing side in the Spanish civil war. Kitty
tried to follow him to Spain, but only got as far as Paris when she
heard that he had been killed in action. Three years later she married Robert. Robert and Kitty were well suited to each other; they
settled down and raised a family and supported each other in sick-
ness and in health, through all Robert's triumphs and tribulations,
until his death. But I often felt that it must have been hard for

Robert, at least in the early years, to be living in a silent ménage à trois with the ghost of a dead hero.

The Spanish war certainly captured Robert's imagination and caused him to become politically engaged. It was easy for Robert and his left-wing friends, viewing the war from a distance of six thousand miles through a screen of righteous indignation, to romanticize and oversimplify. They looked on the war as a simple fight for freedom, a heroic struggle of right against wrong. They did not read George Orwell's *Homage to Catalonia*, the best eye-witness record of the war, written by a man who fought in it as a private soldier and faithfully set down on paper the heroism and the sordidness, the tragedy and the folly. Orwell's book sold poorly in England and was not published in the United States. The right wing disliked Orwell because he was a Socialist, and the left wing disliked him because he told the truth. The truth was too complicated to fit into the ideological categories of left and right. To a man who kept his eyes open and was not afraid to say what he saw, the disasters of the war could not be blamed on one side alone. One of the minor side effects of the war in Spain was that it erased from the minds of left-wing intellectuals the hard-earned lessons of World War I. They saw the Loyalist cause in the Spanish war as clean, heroic, and virtuous. They forgot what Haldane and Wilfred Owen could have told them, that the conditions of twentieth-century warfare tend to make heroism irrelevant. In the romanticized view of the Spanish war which Robert Oppenheimer absorbed from his friends in Berkeley in the late 1930's, the legend of Joe Dallet, the rich man's son who fought on the side of the workers and laid down his life for their cause, fitted naturally into place.

Recently I learned from the historian Richard Polenberg at Cornell some facts about Joe Dallet's life and death. Dallet was unlike the majority of the left-wing intellectuals who flocked to Spain to fight for the Republic. Dallet took soldiering seriously. He believed, like Robert, in discipline. He quickly became an expert on the repair, maintenance, and use of machine guns. He drilled his troops with old-fashioned thoroughness, making sure that they knew how to take care of their weapons and how to use them effectively. In an anarchic situation, his unit was conspicuously well organized. His men caught from him the habit of competence, the pride of a steelworker who knows how to handle machinery. At moments of relaxation, when he sat down with his friends over a bottle of wine, he talked mostly about his beloved machine guns. This was the image of Joe which his friends brought to Kitty in Paris when they came to see her after his death. This was the image which Kitty brought to Robert when she married him.

From Joe's guns it was a short step to Robert's bombs. When Robert accepted in 1942 the job of organizing the bomb laboratory at Los Alamos, it seemed to him natural and appropriate that he should work under the direct command of General Groves of the United States Army. Other leading scientists wanted to keep the laboratory under civilian control. Isadore Rabi was one of those most strongly opposed to working for the Army. Robert wrote to Rabi in February 1943, explaining why he was willing to go with General Groves: "I think if I believed with you that this project was 'the culmination of three centuries of physics,' I should take a different stand. To me it is primarily the development in time of war of a military weapon of some consequence." Rabi did not join the laboratory.

Late in 1944, as the Los Alamos project moved toward success, tensions developed between civilian and military participants. Captain Parsons of the U.S. Navy, serving as associate director under Oppenheimer, complained to him in a written memorandum that some of the civilian scientists were more interested in scientific experiments than in weaponry. Oppenheimer forwarded the memorandum to General Groves, with a covering letter to show which side he himself was on: "I agree completely with all the comments of Captain Parsons' memorandum on the fallacy of regarding a controlled test as the culmination of the work of this laboratory. The laboratory is operating under a directive to produce weapons; this directive has been and will be rigorously adhered to." So vanished the possibility that there might have been a pause for reflection between the Trinity Test and Hiroshima. Captain Parsons, acting in the best tradition of old-fashioned military leadership, flew with the *Enola Gay* to Japan and armed the Hiroshima bomb himself.

Some of the people who worked under Oppenheimer at Los Alamos asked themselves afterwards, "Why did we not stop when the Germans surrendered?" For many of them, the principal motivation for joining the project at the beginning had been the fear that Hitler might get the bomb first. But that danger had disappeared by May 1945 at the latest. So the primary argument which persuaded British and American scientists to go to Los Alamos had ceased to be valid before the Trinity Test. It would have been possible for them to stop. They might at least have paused to ask the question, whether in the new circumstances it was wise to go ahead to the actual production of weapons. Only one man paused. The one who paused was Joseph Rotblat from Liverpool, who, to his everlasting credit, resigned his position at Los Alamos and left the laboratory on May 9, 1945, the day the war in Europe ended. Twelve years later Rotblat helped Bertrand Russell launch the international Pugwash movement; he has remained one of the leaders of Pugwash ever since. The reason why the others did not pause is to be seen clearly in Oppenheimer's assurance to General Groves, written on October 4, 1944: "The Laboratory is operating under a directive to produce weapons; this directive has been and will be rigorously adhered to." Oppenheimer had accepted on behalf of himself and his colleagues the subordination of personal judgment to military authority.

Fighting for freedom. That was the ideal which pulled young men to die in Spain, to take up armed resistance against Hitler in the mountains of Yugoslavia, and to go to work with Oppenheimer in Los Alamos. Fighting for freedom, the traditional and almost instinctive human response to oppression and injustice. Fighting for freedom, the theme song of the Spanish war and of World War II from beginning to end. In 1937 Cecil Day Lewis wrote a war poem called "The Nabara," a long poem, perhaps the only poem which adequately describes the spirit of those who went to fight against hopeless odds in the early battles of World War II, even though it was written before that war started. "The Nabara" is a dirge for fifty-two Spanish fishermen, the crew of an armed trawler which lost a battle against one of Franco's warships. It is also perhaps a dirge for all of us who have chosen to fight for freedom with the technologies of death. I quote here a few of the concluding stanzas:

> Of her officers all but one were dead. Of her engineers
> All but one were dead. Of the fifty-two that had sailed
> In her, all were dead but fourteen, and each of these half
> > killed
> With wounds. And the night-dew fell in a hush of ashen tears,
> > And Nabara's tongue was stilled.

> Canarias lowered a launch that swept in a greyhound's curve
> Pitiless to pursue
> And cut them off. But that bloodless and all-but-phantom
> > crew
> Still gave no soft concessions to fate: they strung their
> > nerve
> For one last fling of defiance, they shipped their oars
> > and threw
> Hand-grenades at the launch as it circled about to board
> > them.
> But the strength of the hands that had carved them a hold
> > on history
> Failed them at last: the grenades fell short of the enemy,
> Who grappled and overpowered them,
> While Nabara sank by the stern in the hushed Cantabrian sea.

They bore not a charmed life. They went into battle
                                                    foreseeing
Probable loss, and they lost. The tides of Biscay flow
Over the obstinate bones of many, the winds are sighing
Round prison walls where the rest are doomed like their
                                            ship to rust,
Men of the Basque country, the Mar Cantábrico.

For these I have told of, freedom was flesh and blood,
                                              a mortal
Body, the gun-breech hot to its touch: yet the battle's
                                              height
Raised it to love's meridian and held it awhile immortal;
And its light through time still flashes like a star's
                                    that has turned to ashes,
Long after Nabara's passion was quenched in the sea's
                                              heart.

Day Lewis published this poem in a little volume with the title
Overtures to Death in 1938. It resonated strongly with the tragic
mood of those days, when the Spanish war was slowly drawing to
its bitter end and the Second World War was inexorably approach-
ing. I remember, when I was at Winchester in 1938, our chemistry teacher Eric James, who was the best teacher in the school,
put aside chemistry for an hour and read "The Nabara" aloud.
He is now, by the way, sitting in the House of Lords. I can still
hear his passionate voice reading "The Nabara," with the boys
listening spellbound. That was perhaps the last occasion on which
it was possible to read an epic poem aloud in all sincerity to honor
the heroes of a military action. At Hiroshima, the new technology
of death made military heroism suddenly old-fashioned and im-
potent. After Hiroshima, Day Lewis's lofty sentiments no longer
resonated. The generation which grew up after Hiroshima found
its voice in 1956 in the character of Jimmy Porter, the young man
at center stage in John Osborne's play *Look Back in Anger*. Here
is Jimmy Porter, griping as usual, and incidentally telling us im-

portant truths about the effect of nuclear weapons on public morality: "I suppose people of our generation aren't able to die for good causes any longer. We had all that done for us, in the thirties and forties, when we were still kids. There aren't any good, brave causes left. If the big bang does come, and we all get killed off, it won't be in aid of the old-fashioned, grand design. It'll just be for the Brave New nothing-very-much-I-thank you. About as pointless and inglorious as stepping in front of a bus."

Jimmy Porter brings us back to where Haldane left us in 1924. The two world wars seemed totally different to the people who fought in them and lived through them from day to day, but they begin to look more and more alike as they recede into history. The first war began with the trumpet-blowing of Rupert Brooke and ended with the nightmares of Wilfred Owen. The second war began with the mourning of Day Lewis and ended with the anger of Jimmy Porter. In both wars, the beginning was young men going out to fight for freedom in a mood of noble self-sacrifice, and the end was a technological bloodbath which seemed in retrospect meaningless. In the first war, the idealism of Rupert Brooke perished and the trench-mortars of Haldane survived; in the second war, the idealism of Joe Dallet perished and the nuclear weapons of Robert Oppenheimer survived. In both wars, history proved that those who fight for freedom with the technologies of death end by living in fear of their own technology.

Oppenheimer's activities as a scholar–soldier did not cease with the end of World War II. After the first Soviet nuclear test in 1949, he took the lead in pushing for a vigorous development of tactical nuclear weapons to be used by the United States Army for the defense of Western Europe. Here is the testimony of his friend Walt Whitman (the chemist, not the poet of that name) as a character witness on Oppenheimer's behalf during the security hearings of 1954:

> I should say that always Dr. Oppenheimer was trying to point out the wide variety of military uses for the bomb, the

small bomb as well as the large bomb. He was doing it in a climate where many folks felt that only strategic bombing was a field for the atomic weapon. I should say that he more than any other man served to educate the military to the potentialities of the atomic weapon for other than strategic bombing purposes; its use possibly in tactical situations or in bombing 500 miles back. He was constantly emphasizing that the bomb would be more available and that one of the greatest problems was going to be its deliverability, meaning that the smaller you could make your bomb in size perhaps you would not have to have a great big strategic bomber to carry it, you could carry it in a medium bomber or you could carry it even in a fighter plane. In my judgment his advice and his arguments for a gamut of atomic weapons, extending even over to the use of the atomic weapon in air defense of the United States, has been more productive than any other one individual.

As a consequence of his interest in tactical nuclear weapons, Oppenheimer traveled to Paris in November 1951 with three other people to talk with General Eisenhower, who was then in command of American forces in Europe. General Eisenhower was quickly persuaded that tactical nuclear weapons would help his armies to carry out their mission of defense. The six thousand NATO tactical warheads now in Europe are an enduring monument to Oppenheimer's powers of persuasion. I once asked him, long after he had lost his security clearance, whether he regretted having fought so hard for tactical nuclear weapons. He said, "No. But to understand what I did then, you would have to see the Air Force war plan as it existed in 1951. That was the Goddamnedest thing I ever saw. Anything, even the war plans we have now, is better than that." The 1951 war plan was, in short, a mindless obliteration of Soviet cities. I could sympathize with Oppenheimer's hatred of the Strategic Air Command mentality, having myself spent two years at the headquarters of the British Bomber Command. I recalled an evening which I spent at the bar of the Bomber Command Officers' Mess, at a time in 1944 when our bombers were still suffering heavy losses in their nightly attacks on German cities. I listened then to a group of drunken headquarters staff-officers discussing the routes they would order their planes to take to Leningrad and Moscow in the war with Russia which they were looking forward to after this little business in Germany was over. Oppenheimer had heard similar talk in his encounters with the American Air Force. Compared with that, even a nucle-arized army seemed to him to be a lesser evil.

Under the circumstances existing in 1951, the idea of tactical nuclear weapons made sense both militarily and politically. The circumstances included a substantial margin of superiority of American over Soviet nuclear forces, both in quantity of weapons and in means of delivery. The circumstances also included a war in Korea, with United States troops fighting hard to defend South Korea against a North Korean invasion supported by the Soviet Union. At that moment of history, Oppenheimer was facing a triple nightmare. He was afraid, first, that the Korean war would spread to Europe; second, that a local invasion of West Berlin or West Germany would be answered by the United States Air Force's 1951 war plan, which meant the nuclear annihilation of Moscow and Leningrad; third, that the surviving Soviet nuclear forces, unable to touch the United States, would take their revenge on Paris and London. It was reasonable to think that the worst part of this nightmare could be avoided if the United States could respond to local invasions with local use of nuclear weapons on the battlefield. Oppenheimer argued in 1951 that the possibility of a restrained and local use of nuclear weapons would strengthen the resolve of Western European governments and enable them to stand firm against Soviet demands. The same arguments for tacti-cal nuclear weapons are still heard today, long after the disap-pearance of the American superiority which made them realistic.

The military doctrine of the NATO alliance is still based upon the possibility of first use of nuclear weapons by the allied armies to counter a Soviet non-nuclear invasion. How far this doctrine

departs from sanity can be vividly seen in the official U.S. Army
field manual FM-101-31-1 on nuclear weapons employment. This
field manual is an unclassified document, used for the training of
United States officers and readily available to foreign intelligence
services. It describes how the well-educated staff-officer should
make his plans during tactical nuclear operations. Various examples are presented of fictitious nuclear engagements, each of them
conducted in a style appropriate to an ROTC Field Day. Here is
"an example of a corps commander's initial guidance to his staff":

> Aggressor has organized the area between our current posi-
> tions and the BLUE River for a determined defense. The deci-
> sive battle during the coming operation will be fought west of
> the BLUE River. Although we have a limited number of
> nuclear weapons for this operation, I am willing to expend
> 30 to 40 percent of our allocation in penetrating the Aggressor
> main and second defense belts, and advancing to the BLUE
> River. Corps fires will be used to engage Aggressor nuclear
> delivery means and those reserve maneuver forces which have
> the capability of adversely affecting the outcome of the battle.
> These fires will be delivered as soon as the targets are located.
> Once we are across the BLUE River, we must be ready to
> exploit our crossings and move rapidly through the passes of
> the SILVER Mountains and seize the communications center of
> FOXVILLE. Be extremely cautious in planning the employment
> of nuclear weapons in the SILVER Mountains, as I want no
> obstacles to our advance created in these critical areas.
> Weapons over 50 KT yield will not be allocated to
> divisions.

The problems of securing adequate intelligence concerning
prospective nuclear targets are also discussed: "Delay of nuclear
attacks until detailed intelligence is developed may impede the
effectiveness of the attack. On the other hand, engagement of a
target without some indication of its characteristics may cause an
unwarranted waste of combat power."

So the staff-officer receiving ambiguous reports of major enemy units moving through populated friendly territory must take upon himself the responsibility of deciding whether to risk "an unwarranted waste of combat power." Fortunately, his task will be made easier by a well-designed system of nuclear bookkeeping. "Suggested forms or methods by which needed information can be kept at various staff agencies are discussed below." Samples are provided of forms to be filled out from time to time, summarizing the numbers of nuclear weapons of various kinds expended and unexpended. Very little is said about the possible disruption of these arrangements by enemy nuclear bombardment. But at least the well-prepared staff-officer knows what to do in one possible contingency. Section 4.17.c on Nuclear Safety reads in its entirety: "Enemy duds are reported to the next higher headquarters."

I ought to apologize to the authors of FM-101-31-1 for holding up their work to ridicule. They lack practical experience of nuclear warfare. When experience is lacking, the handbook-writer does the best he can, using a mixture of commonsense and imagination to fill the gaps in his knowledge. The handbook represents a sincere attempt to put Oppenheimer's philosophy of local nuclear defense into practice. I have taken my quotations from the 1963 edition of FM-101-31-1, the latest edition that I have seen. But when all due allowances are made for the historical context out of which FM-101-31-1 arose, it is still a profoundly disquieting document.

No matter how FM-101-31-1 may have been revised since 1963, it remains true that the doctrines governing the use and deployment of tactical nuclear weapons are basically out of touch with reality. The doctrines are based on the idea that a tactical nuclear operation can be commanded and controlled like an ordinary non-nuclear campaign. This idea may have made sense in the 1950's, but it certainly makes no sense in the 1980's. I have seen the results of computer simulations of tactical nuclear wars under modern conditions, with thousands of warheads deployed on both sides. The computer wars uniformly end in chaos. High-yield weapons are used on a massive scale because nobody knows accurately where the moving targets are. Civilian casualties, if the war is fought in a populated area, are unimaginable. If even the computers are not able to fight a tactical nuclear war without destroying Europe, what hope is there that real soldiers in the fog and flames of a real battlefield could do better?

The doctrines displayed in FM-101-31-1 are doubly dangerous. First, these doctrines deceive our own political leaders, giving them the false impression that tactical nuclear war is a feasible way to defend a country. Second, these doctrines spread around the world and give the military staffs of countries large and small the impression that every army wanting to stay ahead in the modern world should have its own tactical nuclear weapons too. If FM-101-31-1 had been stamped Top Secret it would not have been so harmful. In that case I would not have been talking about it here. But since our military authorities published it unclassified in order to give it a wide distribution, there is no point in trying to keep its existence a secret. The best thing to do in these circumstances is to call attention to its errors and inadequacies, so that people in military intelligence services around the world may not take it too seriously.

Fortunately, leaders of government in the United States and in Europe have come to understand that the purpose of the deployment of tactical nuclear weapons is primarily political rather than military. That is to say, the weapons are deployed as a demonstration of the American political commitment to the NATO alliance, not as a system of military hardware which could actually provide a meaningful defense of Europe. But this separation between political and military purposes of weapons is necessarily hedged about with ambiguities. On the one hand, the political sensitivities of NATO have imposed on the administration of tactical nuclear forces a command structure of unique complexity to ensure that the weapons will not be used irresponsibly. On the other hand, the troops in the field have to be trained and indoctrinated using manuals like FM-101-31-1 which make the firing of nuclear weapons into a standard operating procedure. The whole apparatus for handling tactical nuclear weapons is schizophrenic, trying in vain to accommodate the incompatible requirements of multinational political control and military credibility.

In my opinion, tactical nuclear weapons deployed in forward positions overseas are fundamentally more dangerous to world peace than strategic weapons deployed in silos and in submarines. Tactical weapons are more dangerous for two major reasons. First, tactical weapons are in places where local wars and revolutions may occur, with unpredictable consequences. Second, tactical weapons are deployed, as strategic weapons are not, with a doctrine which allows United States forces to use them first in case of emergency. Many of the tactical weapons are in fact so vulnerable and so exposed that it would make no sense to deploy them in their present positions if the option of first use were renounced. The combination of local political instability with vulnerable weapons and the option of first use is a recipe for disaster. In many ways, it is a situation reminiscent of the Europe of 1914, when the instability of the Hapsburg Empire was combined with vulnerable frontiers and rigid mobilization schedules. Compared with the immediate danger that a local conflict in an area of tactical weapons deployment might escalate into nuclear chaos, the instabilities of the strategic arms race are remote and theoretical.

The United States has already made one important and unilateral move to mitigate the danger of the tactical weapons. The most absurdly dangerous of them all was the Davy Crockett, a nuclear trench-mortar with a low-yield warhead which was supposed to be carried by small mobile units. FM-101-31-1 says (p. 38), "Allocate some Davy Crockett weapons to the cavalry squadron." A nuclear-armed cavalry squadron is a fine example of military euphemism. In reality it meant that Davy Crocketts were deployed in jeeps which were theoretically free to roam around the countryside. The Army decided that this was carrying nuclear dispersal too far. It was impossible to guarantee the physical security of the Davy Crocketts if they were allocated to small units as originally intended. Dispersal in small units also increased substantially the risk of unauthorized firing in case of local hostilities or breakdown of communications. So the Army wisely withdrew the Davy Crocketts from service and shipped them home, achieving thereby a real diminution in the risk of war at no political cost.

The same logic which got rid of the Davy Crocketts would dictate a continued withdrawal, unilateral or bilateral, of other tactical weapons, starting with those which because of their short range have to be deployed closest to the front line. Nuclear artillery shells would be a good candidate for the next round of withdrawals. The chief virtue of nuclear artillery was its high accuracy compared with the rockets of twenty years ago. Now the accuracy of rocket guidance is comparable with the accuracy of artillery. Guns are considerably more cumbersome and more vulnerable than rockets. Nuclear guns have to be placed in forward positions to be effective, they are hard to move quickly, and they are in danger of being overrun whenever there is a local breakthrough of enemy forces. If nuclear shells were not already deployed in our armies overseas, nobody would now dream of introducing them. Their military value is marginal, and they increase the risk that small-scale battles may involve us in unintended nuclear hostilities. They could be withdrawn, like the Davy Crocketts, with a substantial net gain to our security.

It is a strange paradox of history that the greatest present danger of nuclear war arises from these tactical weapons which Oppenheimer promoted with such good intentions during his period of political ascendancy. Oppenheimer pushed tactical nuclear weapons because they offered a counterweight to the Strategic Air Command in the interservice rivalries of the Truman administration, and because they offered a counterweight to Soviet tank armies in case of a war in Western Europe. It is clear that his actions were dominated by short-term considerations. There is no evidence that he ever considered the long-range consequences tactical nuclear weapons would inevitably entail, the massive Soviet response and the permanently increased risk of nuclear war arising by accident or miscalculation.

What are we to learn from this melancholy story? The main lesson, it seems to me, is that if we want to save the world from the horrors of nuclear war we must begin by winning over the soldiers to our side. It is not enough to organize scientists against nuclear war, or physicians against nuclear war, or clergymen against nuclear war, or even musicians against nuclear war. We need captains and generals against nuclear war. We need to persuade the soldiers in all countries, and especially the young men who will be the next generation of military leaders, that they cannot decently fight with nuclear weapons. The elimination of nuclear weapons must be presented to the public as a response to the demands of military honor and self-respect, not as a response to fear.

It is good to make people afraid of nuclear war. But fear is not enough. The generation which grew up after World War I was well indoctrinated in the horrors of trench warfare. Whether or not they read Haldane and Wilfred Owen, they met every day the widows and orphans and crippled survivors of the war. They looked back to the slaughters of Verdun and Passchendaele as we look back to the slaughter of Hiroshima, and they were properly afraid. Pacifist movements flourished in the 1920's and 1930's, and disarmament programs enjoyed wide public support. The fear of a repetition of World War I was real and almost universal. But human beings, for better or for worse, are so constituted that they are not willing to let their lives be ruled for very long by fear. Pride, anger, impatience, and even curiosity are stronger passions than fear. Thousands of men, including one of my uncles, lost their lives in World War I because their curiosity got the better of their fear. They could not resist the urge to stick their heads up out of the trench to see what was happening. Thousands more, including Joe Dallet, lost their lives in a hopeless cause in Spain because their fear was weaker than their anger. There is a deep force in the human spirit which drives us to fight for our freedoms and hang the consequences. Even the fear of nuclear holocaust is not strong enough to prevail against this force. When the trumpets sound and the cause is perceived to be just, young men of spirit, whether they are revolutionaries like Dallet or scholars like Oppenheimer, will lay aside their fears and their misgivings to join the parade, joyfully submitting themselves to the necessities of military discipline; for as Oppenheimer wrote to his brother, "only through them can we attain to the least detachment; and only so can we know peace."

We cannot defeat with fear alone the forces of misguided patriotism and self-sacrifice. We need above all to have sound and realistic military doctrines, doctrines which make clear that the actual use of nuclear weapons cannot either defend our country or defend our allies, that the actual use of nuclear weapons in a world of great powers armed with thousands of warheads cannot serve any sane military purpose whatever. If our military doctrines and plans once recognize these facts, then our military leaders may be able to agree with those of our allies and our adversaries upon practical measures to make the world safer for all of us. If our soldiers once understand that they cannot defend us with nuclear weapons, they may contribute their great moral and political influence to help us create a world in which non-nuclear defense is possible. In England, Lord Mountbatten and Field Marshal Lord Carver have made a good beginning.

The human situation, sitting naked under the threat of nuclear war, is desperate but not hopeless. One hopeful feature of our situation is the demonstrable idiocy of the military plans and deployments typified by Army Field Manual FM-101-31-1. There is a real hope that the soldiers in various countries may rebel against such idiocies and demand a world in which they can fulfill their honorable mission of national defense. The scholar–soldier Robert Oppenheimer persuaded General Eisenhower in 1951 that the American army needed tactical nuclear weapons. The world is now waiting for another scholar–soldier, or for a soldier who is not a scholar, to help us move back along the long road from the illusory world of FM-101-31-1 to a world of sanity.

II. THE QUEST FOR CONCEPT

I borrowed my title "The Quest for Concept" from my Princeton colleague George Kennan. He wrote an essay with this title fifteen years ago. I decided that Kennan's way of looking at things is the best way to come to grips with the problems of nuclear weapons, and so I have adopted Kennan's title as my own. This does not mean that Kennan is responsible for what I shall say. It means that I have accepted Kennan's fundamental standpoint, that we shall not succeed in dealing with the political and technical problems of controlling our weapons until we have agreed upon a coherent concept of what the weapons are for.

Kennan wrote his "Quest for Concept" in 1967, when the Vietnam tragedy was still unfolding and no end was in sight. His final sentences express the hope that sustained him through those dark days, a hope that should also sustain us today as we struggle to deal with the enduring problems of nuclear armaments:

> It remains my hope that if the Vietnam situation takes a turn that permits us once again to conduct our affairs on the basis of deliberate intention rather than just yielding ourselves to be whip-sawed by the dynamics of a situation beyond our control, we will take up once more the quest for concept as a basis for national policy. And I hope that when we do, what we will try to evolve is concept based on a modest unsparing view of ourselves; on a careful examination of our national interest, devoid of all utopian and universalistic pretensions; and upon a sober, discriminating view of the world beyond our

borders — a view that takes account of the element of relativity in all antagonisms and friendships, that sees in others neither angels nor devils, neither heroes nor blackguards; a concept, finally, which accepts it as our purpose not to abolish all violence and injustice from the workings of international society but to confine those inevitable concomitants of the human predicament to levels of intensity that do not threaten the very existence of civilization.

If concept could be based on these principles, if we could apply to its creation the enormous resources of intelligence and ingenuity and sincerity that do exist in this country, and if we could refine it and popularize it through those traditional processes of rational discussion and debate on the efficacy of which, in reality, our whole political tradition is predicated, then I could see this country some day making, as it has never made to date, a contribution to world stability and to human progress commensurate with its commanding physical power.*

Today I shall try to carry forward into the areas of weapons and strategy the process of rational discussion and debate upon which Kennan rested his hope for the future. We now possess weapons of mass destruction whose capacity for killing and torturing people surpasses all our imaginings. The Soviet government has weapons that are as bad or worse. We have been almost totally unsuccessful in halting the multiplication and proliferation of these weapons. Following Kennan's lead, I want to ask some simple questions. What are these weapons for? What are the concepts which drive the arms race, on our side and on the Soviet side? Since the existing concepts have led us into a situation of mortal danger with no escape in sight, can we find any new concepts which might serve our interests better? Can we find a concept of weaponry which would allow us to protect our national interests without committing us to threaten the wholesale massacre of innocent people? Above all, a concept should be robust; robust

* Published as "In American Foreign Policy: The Quest for Concept," in *Harvard To-day* (Autumn 1967), pp. 11–17.

enough to survive mistranslation into various languages, to survive distortion by political pressures and interservice rivalries, to survive drowning in floods of emotion engendered by international crises and catastrophes.

General Sir Archibald Wavell, who commanded British forces in the Middle East in World War II, published an anthology of poetry and also a book on generalship. I quote now from his book on generalship. "Whenever in the old days a new design of mountain gun was submitted to the Artillery Committee, that august body had it taken to the top of a tower, some hundred feet high, and thence dropped onto the ground below. If it was still capable of functioning it was given further trial; if not, it was rejected as flimsy." Wavell remarked that he would like to be allowed to use the same method when choosing a general. His suggestion applies equally well to the choice of strategic concepts. Any concept which is to succeed in regulating the use of weapons must be at least as robust as the weapons themselves or the generals who command them. A test of robustness for a concept, roughly equivalent to Wavell's hundred-foot drop for a mountain gun, is the process of verbal mauling which occurs in the public budgetary hearings of the committees of the United States Senate and House of Representatives.

The present nuclear strategy of the United States is based upon a concept which was definitively stated by Secretary of Defense McNamara in 1967. "The cornerstone of our strategic policy continues to be to deter deliberate nuclear attack upon the United States or its allies by maintaining a highly reliable ability to inflict an unacceptable degree of damage upon any single aggressor or combination of aggressors at any time during the course of a strategic nuclear exchange, even after our absorbing a surprise first strike."

A year earlier, McNamara had given a less formal definition of the concept. "Offensive capability or what I will call the capability for assuring the destruction of the Soviet Union is far and away the most important requirement we have to meet."

The concept is called Assured Destruction because of McNamara's choice of words. It is also sometimes called Mutual Assured Destruction, with the implication that the Russians possess the same capability for destroying us as we possess for destroying them and that Soviet strategy should be based on the same concept as our strategy. I will discuss Soviet strategy a little later. One thing that emerges clearly from Soviet doctrines is that the Soviet Union does not accept Mutual Assured Destruction as a strategic goal. The word mutual is therefore misleading. It is better to call our concept Assured Destruction and to let the Russians speak for themselves.

Assured Destruction has at least the virtue of robustness. McNamara never had any difficulty in explaining it to congressional committees. It survived untouched the Vietnam War and the attendant political upheavals which changed so many other aspects of American life and incidentally put an end to McNamara's tenure as Secretary of Defense. It still survives today as the ruling principle of American weapons deployment and of American conduct of arms-control negotiations. The words "assured destruction" are clear and unambiguous, and their meaning survives translation into Russian. The ability to survive translation is an important virtue. Endless trouble and misunderstanding was caused by the word "deterrence," which is a slippery concept in English and is usually translated into Russian as *ustrashenie*. It turns out that the word *ustrashenie* really means "intimidation," and so it was not surprising that discussions with Russians about deterrence proved frustrating to all concerned. There is no such difficulty with Assured Destruction. Assured Destruction means exactly what it says. It means, no matter what you do and no matter what happens to us, we retain the capability to bomb you back into the Stone Age.

I make a sharp distinction between Assured Destruction as a fact and Assured Destruction as a concept. It is a fact that we can assuredly destroy any country in the world, including our own, any time we feel like it. It is a fact that the Soviet Union can do the same. These are facts with which I have no quarrel. But the concept of Assured Destruction means something else. The concept means that we adopt as the ruling principle of foreign policy the perpetuation of this state of affairs. The concept means that we actively desire and pursue the capability for Assured Destruction, with a priority overriding all other objectives. That is what McNamara said: "Assured Destruction is far and away the most important requirement we have to meet." That is still the concept underlying United States policy today. Assured Destruction must come first; everything else, including our own survival, second. It is this concept of Assured Destruction, making it into the primary objective of our policy, which I wish to challenge. The fact of Assured Destruction is at the moment inescapable. The concept of Assured Destruction as a permanently desirable goal is, to my mind, simply insane.

The new strategic doctrine enunciated by President Carter in Presidential Directive 59 in 1980 does not change this concept. I cannot discuss PD 59 in detail, because I do not know what it says, and I do not even know anybody who has seen the document itself. From Secretary of Defense Brown's description of PD 59 it is clear that it leaves intact the concept of Assured Destruction as the primary purpose of strategic forces. What PD 59 apparently does is to add to assured destruction a number of preliminary stages, so that we can theoretically carry out various "lower-level" nuclear attacks on military and political targets in the Soviet Union while keeping the weapons needed for assured destruction in reserve. It is irrelevant to my argument whether the idea of lower-level nuclear attacks is realistic or illusory. In either case, as Secretary Brown said, the new doctrine describes only an embellishment and not an abandonment of previous concepts.

There are three compelling reasons why we should oppose the concept of Assured Destruction. First, it is immoral. Second, it is in the long run suicidal. Third, it is not shared by the Soviet Union, and therefore it stands in the way of any satisfactory and permanent arms-control agreement. I think I do not need to spell out why it is immoral to base our policy upon the threat to carry out a massacre of innocent people greater than all the massacres in mankind's bloody history. But it may be worthwhile to remind ourselves that a deep awareness of the immorality of our policy is a major contributory cause of the feelings of malaise and alienation which are widespread among intelligent Americans and of the feelings of distrust with which the United States is regarded by people overseas who might have been our friends. An immoral concept is not only bad in itself but also has a corrosive effect upon our spirits. It deprives us of our self-respect and of the good opinion of mankind, two things more important to our survival than invulnerable missiles.

I also do not need to spell out why the concept of Assured Destruction is ultimately suicidal. The concept rests on the belief that, if we maintain under all circumstances the ability to do unacceptable damage to our enemies, our weapons will never be used. We all know that this idea makes sense so long as quarrels between nations are kept under control by statesmen weighing carefully the consequences of their actions. But who, looking at the historical record of human folly and accident which led us into the international catastrophes of the past, can believe that careful calculation and rational decision will prevail in all the crises of the future? Inevitably, if we maintain Assured Destruction as a permanent policy, there will come a time when folly and accident will surprise us again as they surprised us in 1914. And this time the guns of August will be shooting with thermonuclear warheads.

The third defect of Assured Destruction as a concept is that it is not shared by the Soviet Union. Soviet leaders have told us repeatedly in no uncertain terms that they reject it. They have told us that they consider the deliberate destruction of civilian populations to be a barbarous concept and that their strategic forces will never be used for that purpose. I am not an expert on Soviet strategic doctrine, but I think there is good reason to believe that they mean what they say. The counterpart to McNamara's statement of our concept of Assured Destruction is the statement made in 1971 by the Soviet Minister of Defense, the late Marshal Grechko. Here is Marshal Grechko speaking: "The Strategic Rocket Forces, which constitute the basis of the military might of our armed forces, are designed to annihilate the means of the enemy's nuclear attack, large groupings of his armies, and his military bases; to destroy his military industries; and to disorganize the political and military administration of the aggressor as well as his rear and transport."

I am not claiming that Marshal Grechko's concept is gentler or more humane than McNamara's, but it is certainly different. Grechko did not design his forces with the primary mission of doing unacceptable damage to our society. Their primary mission is to put our military forces out of action as rapidly and as thoroughly as possible. Unacceptable damage to our population will be a probable consequence of their use, but it is not their main purpose. The technical name for Marshal Grechko's concept is Counterforce. Counterforce means that your ultimate purpose is to ensure the survival of your own society by destroying the enemy's weapons. Your immediate objective is to disarm him, not to destroy him.

There are many cultural and historical reasons why the counterforce concept fits better into the Russian than into the American way of thinking about war. The first and most important fact to remember about Russian generals is that they start out by reading Tolstoy's *War and Peace*. Their whole experience of war and peace in the years since 1914 has confirmed the truth of Tolstoy's vision. War according to Tolstoy is a desperate chaos, largely beyond human understanding and human control. In spite of terrible blunders and terrible losses, the Russian people in the end win by virtue of their superior discipline and powers of endurance.

All this is entirely alien to the American view of thermonuclear war as a brief affair, lasting a few hours or days, with the results predictable in advance by a computer calculation like a baseball score, so many megadeaths on one side and so many megadeaths on the other. Assured destruction makes sense if war is short, calculable, and predictable. Counterforce makes sense if war is long-drawn-out and unpredictable, and the best you can do is to save as many lives as you can and go on fighting with whatever you have left. I happen to believe that the Russian view of war, being based on a longer historical experience, is closer to the truth than ours. That is not to say that their concept of counterforce is free of illusions. Neither assured destruction nor counterforce is to me an acceptable concept. If I had to make a choice between them, I would choose counterforce as less objectionable on moral grounds. But neither assured destruction nor counterforce answers our most urgent need, which is to find a concept which both sides can understand and accept as a basis for arms-control negotiations.

The tragedy of the SALT negotiations, in my opinion, arose out of the basic incompatibility of the American and Soviet strategic concepts. The Soviet concept of counterforce says, "whatever else happens, if you drive us to war, we shall survive." The American concept of assured destruction says, "whatever else happens, if you drive us to war, you shall not survive." It is impossible to find, even theoretically, any arrangement of strategic forces on the two sides which satisfies both these demands simultaneously. That is why no satisfactory treaty can emerge from arms control negotiations so long as the concepts on the two sides remain as they are. The SALT II treaty was better than no treaty at all, but it was a miserable thing, unloved even by its friends, demonstrating the bankruptcy of the strategic concepts that gave it birth. If that is the best that our present concepts can do for us, then let us in God's name look for some better concepts.

When one contemplates the barbarity and insanity of our existing weapons and the plans for their further multiplication, one is tempted to say that there is no hope of salvation in any concept that does not reject them unconditionally. Perhaps it is true that we would be better off rejecting nuclear weapons unilaterally and unconditionally, irrespective of what other countries may decide to do. But unilateral disarmament is not by itself a sufficient basis for a foreign policy. Unilateral disarmament needs to be supplemented by a concept stating clearly what we are to do after we have disarmed, if we are confronted by hostile powers making unacceptable demands. There is a concept which deals with this question in a morally and intellectually consistent way, namely the concept of nonviolent resistance. Nonviolent resistance is not the same thing as surrender. Morally, nonviolent resistance and surrender are at opposite poles. The concept of nonviolent resistance says simply: "You shall not obey unjust laws, you shall not collaborate with unjust authorities, and you shall not shed any man's blood except your own."

Everybody who thinks seriously about nuclear weapons must sooner or later face in his own conscience the question whether nonviolence is or is not a practical alternative to the path we are now following. Is nonviolence a possible basis for the foreign policy of a great country like the United States? Or is it only a private escape-route available to religious minorities who are protected by a majority willing to fight for their lives? I do not know the answers to these questions. I do not believe that anybody knows the answers.

Gandhi in the 1930's made nonviolent resistance the basis of an effective political campaign against British rule in India. All of us young Englishmen who were against the Establishment and against the Empire acclaimed Gandhi as a hero, and many of us became believers in his concept of nonviolence. Then came Hitler. Hitler presented us with a dilemma. On the one hand, we still believed theoretically in the ethic of nonviolence. On the other hand, we looked at what was happening in Europe and said, "But unfortunately nonviolent resistance will not be effective against

Hitler." So in the end, almost all of us abandoned our allegiance to nonviolence and went to war against Hitler. It seemed to us at the time that there was no effective alternative to guns and bombs if we wanted to preserve our lives and liberty. Most people today would say that we were right.

Now, forty years later, a book called *Lest Innocent Blood Be Shed* has been written by Philip Hallie, telling the story of a French village which chose the path of nonviolent resistance to Hitler.* It is a remarkable story. It shows that nonviolence could be effective, even against Hitler. The village of Le-Chambon-sur-Lignon collectively sheltered and saved the lives of many hundreds of Jews through the years when the penalty for this crime was deportation or death. The villagers were led by their Protestant pastor André Trocmé, who had been for many years a believer in nonviolence and had prepared them mentally and spiritually for this trial of strength. When the Gestapo raided the village from time to time, Trocmé's spies usually gave him enough warning so that the refugees could be hidden in the woods. German authorities arrested and executed various people who were known to be leaders in the village, but the resistance continued unbroken. The only way the Germans could have crushed the resistance was by deporting or killing the entire population. Nearby, in the same part of France, there was a famous regiment of SS troops, the Tartar Legion, trained and experienced in operations of extermination and mass brutality. The Tartar Legion could easily have exterminated Le Chambon. But the village survived. Even Trocmé himself, by a series of lucky accidents, survived.

Many years later Trocmé discovered how it happened that the village had survived. The fate of the village was decided in a dialogue between two German soldiers, representing precisely the bright and the dark sides of the German soul. On the one side, Colonel Metzger — an appropriate name meaning in German

* *Lest Innocent Blood Be Shed: The Story of the Village of Le Chambon and How Goodness Happened There* (New York: Harper and Row, 1979).

"Butcher" — commander of the Tartar Legion, killer of civilians, executed after the liberation of France as a war criminal. On the other side, Major Schmehling, Bavarian Catholic and decent German officer of the old school. Both Metzger and Schmehling were present at the trial of Le Forestier, a medical doctor in Le Chambon who was arrested and executed as an example to the villagers. "At his trial," said Schmehling, when he met Trocmé many years later, "I heard the words of Dr. Le Forestier, who was a Christian and explained to me very clearly why you were all disobeying our orders in Le Chambon. I believed that your doctor was sincere. I am a good Catholic, you understand, and I can grasp these things . . . . Well, Colonel Metzger was a hard one, and he kept on insisting that we move in on Le Chambon. But I kept telling him to wait. I told Metzger that this kind of resistance had nothing to do with violence, nothing to do with anything we could destroy with violence. With all my personal and military power I opposed sending his legion into Le Chambon."

That was how it worked. It was a wonderful illustration of the classic concept of nonviolent resistance. You, the doctor Le Forestier, die for your beliefs, apparently uselessly. But your death reaches out and touches your enemies, so that they begin to behave like human beings. Some of your enemies, like Major Schmehling, are converted into friends. And finally even the most hardened and implacable of your enemies, like the SS colonel, are persuaded to stop their killing. It happened like that, once upon a time, in Le Chambon.

What did it take to make the concept of nonviolent resistance effective? It took a whole village of people, standing together with extraordinary courage and extraordinary discipline. Not all of them shared the religious faith of their leader, but all of them shared his moral convictions and risked their lives every day to make their village a place of refuge for the persecuted. They were united in friendship, loyalty, and respect for one another.

So I come back to the question: what would it take to make the concept of nonviolent resistance into an effective basis for the

policy of a country? It would take a whole country of people
standing together with extraordinary courage and extraordinary
discipline. Can we find such a country in the world as it is today?
Perhaps we can, among countries which are small and homogene-
ous and possess a long tradition of quiet resistance to oppression.
But how about the United States? Can we conceive of nonviolent
resistance as an effective concept for the foreign policy of the
United States? Reluctantly I have to answer this question in the
negative. Nonviolence is a noble concept, and in many domestic
situations within the United States, a practical concept, as Martin
Luther King and others have demonstrated. But for the guiding
concept of American foreign policy, nonviolent resistance lacks the
essential quality of robustness. It could never survive the shock of
a major international crisis, nor even the sniping of congressional
committees going about their political business as usual.

I led you into this digression and spoke about André Trocmé
and Le Chambon because I consider that our existing weapons and
concepts are morally unacceptable and that every possible alternative road, no matter how radical or impractical, ought to be ex-
amined carefully. The digression is now at an end. Reluctantly I
have to end the discussion of nonviolence, so far as United States
foreign policy is concerned, with the question which Bernard Shaw
puts at the end of his play *Saint Joan*:

> O God that madest this beautiful earth,
> when will it be ready to receive Thy
> Saints? How long, O Lord, how long?

I come back to the main road, the Street without Joy of national nuclear policies. I am trying to find a middle way between
the concepts of Assured Destruction and nonviolent resistance,
between Robert McNamara and André Trocmé. I believe there is
such a middle way, and I believe my friend Donald Brennan knew
roughly where it lies. Donald Brennan, alas, died two years ago at
the age of fifty-four. I quote now from his testimony to the House

Foreign Affairs Committee of the U.S. Congress on July 17, 1969: "Let us consider two principles. The first principle is that, following any Soviet attack, we should be able to do at least as badly to the Soviets as they had done to us." Donald Brennan liked to call this principle the "Brass Rule," meaning that it is a debased form of the Golden Rule which says you should do unto others what you wish they would do unto you. Note that this principle does not require us to do very badly unto the Soviets if they cannot do very badly unto us.

"The second principle is that we should prefer live Americans to dead Russians, whenever a choice between the two presents itself. The Soviets may be expected to prefer live Russians to dead Americans, and therein resides the basis for an important common interest; we may both prefer live Americans and live Russians." Brennan ends by explaining why his second principle, the preference for live Americans over dead Russians, is controversial. It is controversial because it says that Assured Destruction is not desirable as a way of life. Assured Destruction may be necessary when no alternative is available, but we should not prefer it.

The concept which Donald Brennan advocated is called by the experts in arms control "Parity plus Damage-Limiting." I prefer to call it "Live-and-Let-Live." Perhaps it may be important to use a name for it which the public can understand. Donald Brennan was unfortunately an experts' expert, expressing his strategic concept in technical language which had little public impact. I believe the name "Live-and-Let-Live" accurately describes his concept and does not conceal its profound moral implications. To summarize Brennan's statement once again, his concept says: "We maintain the ability to damage you as badly as you can damage us, but we prefer our own protection to your destruction." I believe that this concept fits, as Assured Destruction does not, George Kennan's requirement that a concept should be modest, unpretentious, and free from apocalyptic overtones.

Live-and-Let-Live is a concept which should rule over all areas of our foreign policy, not only over the technical issues of the strategic arms race. Live-and-Let-Live should have a major impact on the weapons which we and our allies deploy in Western Europe and on the political problems which surround the control and use of these weapons. The tactical nuclear weapons in Western Europe make sense only as a component of an Assured Destruction strategy. If they are ever used, they will bring Assured Destruction immediately to Western Europe and with high probability to the Soviet Union and the United States too. The Live-and-Let-Live concept implies that we no longer regard tactical nuclear weapons as a satisfactory solution to the problem of European security. The ultimate objective of our policy must be to get rid of tactical nuclear weapons altogether. I have no illusion that we can get rid of tactical nuclear weapons quickly or easily. I am saying only that it is an even greater illusion to imagine that we can go on living with them forever.

Two technical factors ought to help us to move toward a Live-and-Let-Live strategy in Europe. First, our professional soldiers recognize the cumbersomeness of the nuclear weapon command structure and the extreme vulnerability of the whole tactical nuclear weapon apparatus to a Soviet preemptive strike. Second, the development of precision-guided munitions — which is the technical name for small, cheap, accurate, non-nuclear missiles capable of destroying tanks and airplanes — offers a realistic substitute for tactical nuclear weapons in the defense of Europe against a Soviet invasion. It is quite wrong to claim, as some enthusiasts for precision-guided munitions have claimed, that these are magic weapons which will solve our military problems in Europe overnight. There are no magic weapons. But there are good as well as bad military technologies. A good military technology is one which leads away from weapons of mass destruction toward weapons which allow people to defend their homeland against invasion without destroying it. The technology of precision-guided munitions is good in this sense. It is reasonable to imagine a hopeful evolution of affairs in Europe, with the technology evolving away from nuclear weapons toward precision-guided non-nuclear weapons, and with the political authorities evolving away from Assured Destruction toward Live-and-Let-Live. Technical and political development must go hand in hand, each helping the other along.

The defense of Western Europe lies at the heart of our fatal involvement with nuclear weapons. Both tactical and strategic nuclear forces grew up in the context of the military confrontation between East and West in Europe. It is important to understand the difference between the Eastern and the Western concepts of nuclear weapons as they relate to the European situation. And it is important to understand the difference between the concepts of first use and first strike. The American doctrine says that we are prepared to use tactical nuclear weapons first if this is necessary to stop a non-nuclear invasion of Western Europe, but we do not contemplate using strategic weapons first in a direct attack on the Soviet Union. That is to say, American doctrine allows first use but forbids first strike. Soviet doctrine says that the Soviet Union will never be the first to introduce nuclear weapons into a non-nuclear war, but that the Soviet Union is prepared to respond to any Western use of tactical nuclear weapons on the battlefield with a strategic attack on the United States and its allies. That is to say, Soviet doctrine forbids first use but allows first strike. There are good and valid geographical reasons why first use seems good to us and bad to them while first strike seems good to them and bad to us. Unfortunately, the general public and the politicians on both sides do not understand the difference. Our people feel threatened when they hear that Russian doctrine allows first strike, and the Russians feel threatened when they hear that our doctrine allows first use.

What hope is there of escape from this web of threats and misunderstandings? A useful first step would be to educate the public so that the public knows the difference between first use and first strike. After that, it might be possible to discuss strategic doctrines publicly with some degree of rationality. Ultimately, we might be able to negotiate some kind of bargain with the Soviet Union in which we agree to give up the capability for first use while they give up the capability for first strike. A trade-off of first use against first strike capabilities would not only improve the security of both sides but would also, more importantly, diminish the psychological anxieties which drive the arms race. Such a trade-off should certainly be one of the immediate objectives of a Live-and-Let-Live strategy.

George Kennan has been the most thoughtful and consistent opponent of our first use doctrine, and I am delighted to see in a recent issue of *Foreign Affairs* that McNamara has publicly joined him in opposition to First Use. "I would submit," Kennan wrote in 1959, "that the first thing we have to do in order to put ourselves in a position to negotiate hopefully for an abolition of nuclear weapons, or indeed to have any coherent strategy of national defense, is to wean ourselves from this fateful and pernicious principle of first use." Kennan's words are as true now as they were twenty-three years ago. A simple No-First-Use declaration by the United States would be of enormous importance in lessening the risk of the outbreak of nuclear war. Recently a distinguished panel of military experts contemptuously dismissed the idea of a No-First-Use declaration on the ground that "declarations like that get put aside in the first moments of conflict." This shows that the panel did not understand what a No-First-Use declaration is designed to do. The purpose of a No-First-Use declaration is not to constrain the use of weapons in wartime but to constrain the deployment of weapons in peacetime. When Country A signs a No-First-Use declaration, the effect is to force the military authorities in Country A to take into account the possibility that the political authorities in Country A may actually mean what they say. This means that Country A is forced to go to the trouble of hardening and concealing its weapons or withdraw-

ing them from exposed positions where they would be vulnerable
to preemptive attack. The effect is to make Country A's deployments more survivable and at the same time less threatening to
neighboring countries. The risk of war is reduced by these changes
in peacetime deployments, not by any possible direct effect of a
No-First-Use declaration in wartime.

Now suppose that two hostile countries A and B both sign a
No-First-Use declaration. The effectiveness of the declaration in
constraining Country A's deployments does not depend at all upon
Country A believing that Country B is sincere. On the contrary,
the more Country A mistrusts Country B's intentions, the stronger
the effect of the declaration in discouraging Country A from un-
stable deployments. For the declaration to be effective, it is necessary only that Country A considers Country B not entirely trust-
worthy and Country A not entirely untrustworthy and vice versa.
These conditions are rather well satisfied in the real world in
which we are living.

The practical relevance of these considerations is most clearly
seen in the contrast between U.S. deployment policies for strategic
and tactical weapons. The U.S. strategic forces are deployed under
our No-First-Strike policy, with the result that there is strong
emphasis on hardening and concealment. Our tactical nuclear
weapons in Europe and elsewhere are not subject to No-First-Use
constraints, with the result that they are far more exposed and
vulnerable. I believe that the tactical weapons are more likely than
the strategic weapons to get us into bad trouble, and I believe that
a No-First-Use declaration covering the tactical nuclear weapons
of the NATO alliance would substantially reduce the danger of
nuclear war. Of course, a NATO No-First-Use declaration would
imply a drastic change in NATO force-structure and strategy,
which just goes to show that the declaration would not be as
empty of meaning as the panel of military experts supposed.

But I will not digress further into the complexities of First
Use and First Strike. Let me come back to the strategic weapons.

I must try to tell you briefly what Live-and-Let-Live means for our strategic policy. First of all, it means no MX. And it means not just saying no to the Racetrack deployment of MX, but saying no to the MX missile in any shape or form. MX is a big step in the wrong direction from almost every point of view. But the question whether or not we deploy a particular weapon such as the MX is not the crucial issue. The far more important consequence of the Live-and-Let-Live concept is that it allows us, or rather compels us, to reorient our deployment strategies and our negotiating policies so that we are prepared in principle to go all the way to a world from which nuclear weapons have been eliminated entirely. So long as we stay with the concept of Assured Destruction, we cannot even contemplate negotiating the numbers of nuclear weapons all the way down to zero; we cannot even offer to our grandchildren any realistic hope of living in a non-nuclear world. The essence of the Live-and-Let-Live concept is that it releases us from inevitable and permanent dependence upon nuclear weapons. It allows us to work toward a future in which strategic offensive deployments are drastically reduced or altogether prohibited. It allows us to prepare in a realistic way to deal with the problems of international security in a non-nuclear world.

To achieve agreements drastically reducing numbers of offensive weapons, and to provide some assurance against clandestine violations, a deployment of non-nuclear missile defenses is likely to be helpful. In the long run, the transition from a world of Assured Destruction to a world of Live-and-Let-Live must be accompanied by a transfer of emphasis from offensive to defensive weapons. When we are talking about defensive weapons in general and about ballistic missile defense in particular, it is essential to make a sharp distinction between ends and means. Our experts in the arms control community have never maintained this distinction. They are so convinced of the technical superiority of offensive over defensive weapons that they let the means determine the ends. I say that we have no hope of escape from the trap we are in unless we follow ends which are ethically acceptable. The end must determine the means, and not vice versa. The only acceptable end that I can see, short of a disarmed world, is a non-nuclear and defensively-oriented world. Perhaps we may be lucky enough to jump to the disarmed world without going through the intermediate step of a defensive world. But at least we ought to consider seriously the question whether the defensive world is an end worth striving for. This question must come first. Only afterwards comes the question of means.

Defense is not technically sweet. The primal sin of scientists and politicians alike has been to run after weapons which are technically sweet. Why must arms-controllers fall into the same trap? There is a terrible arrogance in the statement that defense is hopeless and should therefore be forbidden. Nobody can possibly foresee the state of the world ten years ahead, let alone fifty. If a defensively-oriented world is an end worth striving for, and if we pursue it diligently with all the available means, especially with moral and political as well as technical means, we have a good chance of success. The burden is on the opponents of defense to prove that a defensive world is politically impossible. It is not enough for them to say, we didn't solve the decoy discrimination problem.

Opponents of defense often claim that a defensive strategy is unfeasible because defensive weapons don't work. Whether this claim is valid depends on what we mean by the word "work." If we mean by "work" that a weapon should save our lives in the event of a nuclear war, then defensive weapons do not work and offensive weapons do not work either. If we mean by "work" that a weapon should save those targets which are not attacked, then defensive weapons work very well and offensive weapons do too. In the real world the question whether weapons "work" is equally ambiguous and uncertain, whether the weapons are offensive or defensive. We cannot be sure that weapons of any kind will save our skins if worst comes to worst. We cannot be sure that either defensive or offensive weapons will be useless in discouraging madmen from murdering their neighbors. So there are no compelling technical grounds for choosing an offensive rather than a defensive strategy as a basis for our long-term security. The choice ought to be made on political and moral grounds. Technology is a good servant but a bad master. If we decide on moral grounds that we choose a non-nuclear defense-dominated world as our long-range objective, the political and technological means for reaching the objective will sooner or later be found, whether the means are treaties and doctrines or radars and lasers.

I have described in very brief and inadequate fashion some possible steps by which we might move from a nuclear offensive-dominated world to a non-nuclear defensive-dominated world, from a world of Assured Destruction to a world of Live-and-Let-Live. This great and difficult transition could only be consummated if both the United States and the Soviet Union were to adopt the Live-and-Let-Live concept as the basis of their policies. As we know from Marshal Grechko and others, the Soviet Union at present believes in Counterforce and not in Live-and-Let-Live. That is to say, the Soviet Union in general prefers to be able to destroy our weapons rather than to defend itself against them. It is likely that the Soviet preference for counterforce will last for some time. So long as the Soviet Union stays with the counterforce concept, we shall not achieve a defense-dominated world. But even now, we shall be in a safer and more stable situation if we unilaterally move to a Live-and-Let-Live policy than if we stay with Assured Destruction. For us to adopt unilaterally a Live-and-Let-Live concept does not mean that we let down our strategic guard or that we put our trust in Soviet good will or that we change our opinions of the nature of Soviet society. It merely means that we change the primary objective of our strategic deployment from the Assured Destruction of Soviet society to the Assured Survival of our own.

I would like to end as I began with some words of hope. I shall quote again from the essay of George Kennan which gave

me the theme for this lecture. Kennan is describing the concept
which he advocated as a basis for a rational American foreign
policy in the years immediately following the Second World War.

> We in the Planning Staff were concerned to restore an ade-
> quate balance of power in Europe and eventually in Asia. We
> thought that once such a balance had been restored, we would
> negotiate a military and political Soviet retirement from Cen-
> tral Europe in return for a similar retirement on our part. We
> saw no virtue in keeping our military forces nose to nose with
> those of Russia. We welcomed the prospect of the emergence,
> between Russia and ourselves, of a Europe that would be
> neither an extension of Soviet military power nor of our own.
> We thought all this could be achieved by indirect, political
> means. It was our hope that if we could make progress along
> the lines I have described, there would be a good chance that
> the world would be carried successfully through the crisis of
> instability flowing from the defeat of Germany and Japan.
> New vistas might later open up — vistas not visible at that
> time — for the employment of our great national strength to
> constructive and hopeful ends.

This concept is still as valid today as it was in 1947. And today
it carries with it an even greater promise, the promise of a first
decisive step back from our fatal addiction to the technology
of death.

III. TRAGEDY AND COMEDY IN MODERN DRESS

I begin with a quick summary of the first two lectures. In the
first lecture I described the central tragedy of our century, the history of the two World Wars. I told how in both wars the just
cause with which the war began, the fight for freedom, was corrupted and almost obliterated by the growth of the modern technology of killing. The culmination of this history was the development of nuclear weapons in quantities so large as to obliterate any

conceivable just cause in which they might be used. Nevertheless, the cultural patterns of the past persist, and the safeguards regulating the use of these weapons are not proof against technical accidents and human folly. In the second lecture I discussed the concepts underlying our strategic doctrines and reached the conclusion that a concept which I call Live-and-Let-Live offers the best chance of escape from the predicament in which we are now caught. The essence of the Live-and-Let-Live concept is a determination to move as rapidly as possible away from offensive and nuclear weaponry towards defensive and non-nuclear weaponry. The means for bringing about this movement are moral, political, and technical, in that order. Morally, we must arouse the conscience of mankind against weapons of mass murder as we roused mankind against the institution of slavery a hundred and fifty years ago. Politically, we must negotiate international agreements to reduce offensive deployments and strengthen defensive capabilities. Technically, we must push further the development of non-nuclear defensive systems which may enhance the stability of a non-nuclear world.

This third lecture is concerned not with details of weapons but with human psychology and human values. I must apologize for disappointing those of you who may have been expecting me to provide a political program for the cure of the world's ills. I am not a politician and I have no program. I believe there is a chance that we may now be at a historical turning-point, with mankind as a whole beginning to turn decisively against nuclear weapons. If this turning is real, it will find appropriate political forms in which to express itself. If the turning is not real, no political program can succeed in bringing us to nuclear disarmament. So I decided in my last lecture to follow the wishes of Mr. Tanner and talk about humanity and morality rather than about weapons and politics. This has the consequence that I shall be talking today on a more personal level than before. I cannot discuss human values in the abstract but only in terms of particular people and particular events. I shall talk mostly about American people and American events, because America has been my home for thirty years and I prefer to speak of things which I know from first-hand experience.

Napoleon said that in war the moral factors are to the material factors as ten to one. The same ratio between moral and material factors should hold good in our struggle to abolish nuclear weapons. That is why I said that the moral conviction must come first, the political negotiations second, and the technical means third in moving mankind toward a hopeful future. The first and most difficult step is to convince people that movement is possible, that we are not irremediably doomed, that our lives have a meaning and a purpose, that we can still choose to be masters of our fate.

Polls taken among young people in American schools and colleges in recent years have shown that a consistently large majority believe, on the one hand, that their lives are likely to end in a nuclear war, and on the other hand, that there is no point in worrying about it since it is bound to happen anyway. We are all to some extent affected by this paralysis of the will, this atrophy of the moral sense. We shrug off with silly excuses our burden of responsibility for the impending tragedy. We behave like the characters in a Samuel Beckett play, sitting helplessly in our dustbins while the endgame of history is played out. Or we fritter away our days like John Osborne's Jimmy Porter, waiting for the big bang to come and convinced that nothing can be done about it, accepting the inevitability of a holocaust which is, as Jimmy says, "about as pointless and inglorious as stepping in front of a bus." Why have we become so apathetic and fatalistic? What is wrong with us? The subject of my third lecture will be the restoration of a sense of meaning to the modern world. If we can recover a sense of meaning, then we may also find the moral strength to tackle the institution of nuclear weaponry as resolutely as our ancestors tackled the institution of slavery.

The first step toward dealing effectively with the problem of meaninglessness in modern life is to recognize that it is nothing new. When the difficulties of modern living are discussed in magazines and on television, we often hear statements implying that our generation is unique, that never before in history did people have to cope with such rapid changes in social and moral standards, and so on. If people believe that their difficulties are new and never happened before, then they are deprived of the enormous help which the experience of past generations can provide. They do not take the trouble to learn how their parents and grandparents struggled with similar difficulties. They never acquire the long perspective of history which would let them see the littleness of their own problems in comparison with the problems of the past. If people lack a sense of proportion and a sense of kinship with past generations, then it is not surprising that they become anxious and confused and fall into the mood of self-pity which is one of the most unattractive aspects of the contemporary scene.

The beginning of a cure for this disease is to convince the patient that, as a matter of historical fact, past generations were as troubled as we are by the psychological disorientation associated with rapid change. I could give many examples to prove it, but since time is limited I will give only one. I ask you to consider the Pilgrim Fathers at Plymouth in Massachusetts, three hundred and fifty years ago. We all have a mental image of the society in which the Pilgrims lived after they settled in New England. The village clustered around the church, the hard work in the fields, the shared privations and dangers, the daily prayers, the old-fashioned puritan virtues, the simple faith in divine providence, the ceremony of thanksgiving after harvest. Surely here was a society that was at peace with itself, a community close-knit through personal friendships and religious loyalties. This traditional image of the Pilgrim society is not entirely false. But the reality is stranger and more complicated.

Here is the reality. William Bradford, passenger in the *May-flower* and historian of the Plymouth colony, is writing in the year 1632, twelve years after the first landing.

> Also the people of the Plantation began to grow in their outward estates, by reason of the flowing of many people into the country, especially into the Bay of the Massachusetts. By which means corn and cattle rose to a great price, by which many were much enriched and commodities grew plentiful. And yet in other regards this benefit turned to their hurt, and this accession of strength to their weakness. For now as their stocks increased and the increase vendible, there was no longer any holding them together, but now they must of necessity go to their great lots . . . . By which means they were scattered all over the Bay quickly, and the town in which they lived compactly till now was left very thin and in a short time almost desolate.

So you see, suburban sprawl and urban decay were already rampant within twelve years of the beginning. But let me go on with Bradford's account.

> To prevent any further scattering from this place and weakening of the same, it was thought best to give out some good farms to special persons that would promise to live at Plymouth, and likely to be helpful to the church or commonwealth, and so tie the lands to Plymouth as farms for the same; and there they might keep their cattle and tillage by some servants and retain their dwellings here. . . . But alas, this remedy proved worse than the disease; for within a few years those that had thus got footing there rent themselves away, partly by force and partly wearing the rest with importunity and pleas of necessity, so as they must either suffer them to go or live in continual opposition and contention. And others still, as they conceived themselves straitened or to want accommodation, broke away under one pretence or other, thinking their own conceived necessity and the example of others a warrant sufficient for them. And this I fear will be the ruin of New England, at least of the churches of God there, and will provoke the Lord's displeasure against them.

So I leave William Bradford, already in 1632 lamenting the breakdown of the old moral standards and the disintegrating effects of rapid economic growth. The remarkable thing is that these people who broke away from the Plymouth community were not yet the rebellious sons and daughters of the Pilgrims. The sons and daughters had not even had time to grow up. These people who broke away were the Pilgrims themselves, corrupted within twelve years of their landing by the temptations of easy money.

I conclude from this example and from many others that the psychological confusion and shifting values of the modern world are not new. Even the speed with which values shift is not new. Except in a few particularly stable and sheltered societies, moral standards have usually been in turmoil, and our psychological reference-points have rarely endured for longer than a single generation.

The next question is now: granted that past generations shared our problems, what can past generations do to help us? The most helpful thing they did was to leave us their literature. Through the writings of the war poets we can share and understand the meaning of the agonies of the two World Wars. Literature ties us together. Through literature we can know our roots. Through literature we become friends and colleagues of our predecessors. Through literature they talk to us of their troubles and confusions and give us courage to deal with our own. William Bradford understood this very well. His purpose in writing his history of the Plymouth colony was, as he says, "that their children may see with what difficulties their fathers wrestled in going through these things in their first beginnings; and how God brought them along, notwithstanding all their weaknesses and infirmities. As also that some use may be made hereof in after times by others in such like weighty employments." Bradford also understood that if his account was to be useful to future generations it must be totally honest. That is the greatness of Bradford. He shows us the Pilgrims as they really were, not a group of pious saints but a bunch of people like ourselves, mixed-up in their motives and purposes, feuding and quarreling with one another, keeping one eye on heaven and the other eye on the cash-box, and finally, in spite of all their muddles and mistakes, building a new civilization in the wilderness. Proudly Bradford tells how in the eighteenth year of the settlement, standing firm against the murmuring of the rude and ignorant, they hanged three Englishmen for the murder of an Indian.

If we are searching for meaning in a world of shifting standards, literature is one place where we can find it. Meaning is a subtle and elusive quality. It cannot be dished out to patients like a medicine. It is a matter of feeling, not of fact. All of us have periods in our lives when meaning is lost, and other periods when it is found again. It is an inescapable part of the human condition to be constantly borrowing meaning from one another. No man is an island. Or as William Blake said it:

> The bird a nest,
> The spider a web,
> Man friendship.

If we are lucky, we have friends or children or wives or husbands to lend us meaning when we cannot find it for ourselves. But often there come bad times when there are more borrowers than lenders, when a whole society becomes demoralized and finds meaning to be in short supply. Perhaps the present is such a time. In such times, those of us who have a taste for reading can turn to literature and borrow meaning from the past. Literature is the great storehouse where the meanings distilled by all kinds of people out of all kinds of human experience are preserved. From this storehouse we are all free to borrow. Not everybody, of course, reads books. Some cannot read and others prefer television. But there are still enough of us who love literature and know how to find meaning in it, so that we can take care of the needs of the rest by lending out what we have found.

Let me turn now to another writer, closer to us than William Bradford. Some of you in the audience may have had occasion to read a book called *The Siege* by Clara Park of Williamstown, Massachusetts.* Some of you may also have been lucky enough, as I have been, to know Clara Park personally. If I have any wisdom to share with you today, if I have anything to say worth saying on the subject of human values, I owe most of it to her. *The Siege* is the story of the first eight years of the life of Clara Park's autistic daughter. In the book the daughter is called Elly. It is a book about a particular autistic child and her family. And it is also, indirectly, a book about people in general and their search for meaning. We are still quite ignorant of the nature and causes of autism, but we know at least this much. The autistic child is deficient in those mental faculties which enable us to attach meaning to our experiences. We all from time to time have difficulty in grasping the meanings of things which happen to us. The autistic child has the same difficulty in an extreme degree. So the siege by which Clara and her husband and her three older children battered their way into Elly's mind was only an extreme case of the struggle which every teacher must wage to reach the minds of his pupils. The task is the same, to bring a sense of the meaning of life to minds which have lost an awareness of meaning or never possessed it. The story of Clara's siege has many connections with the theme of human response to nuclear weapons. The metaphor of a siege is a good one to describe the struggle we are engaged in. We are trying to surround the sterile official discussions of nuclear strategy with an aroused public concern, to break down the walls of hopelessness and indifference which keep us from feeling the urgency of our danger. Clara is telling us that the search for human values is a two-sided thing. We must be borrowers as well as lenders. The measure of Clara's achievement is that she not

* *The Siege: The First Eight Years of an Autistic Child; With an Epilogue, Fifteen Years Later* (Boston: Little, Brown and Co., 1982). Earlier editions were published in 1967 and 1972.

only planted in Elly's meaningless solitude an understanding of
the meaning of human contact and conversation, but also distilled
out of Elly's illness insights which gave added meaning to her own
life, to the life of her family, and to her work as a teacher.

But I did not come here to praise Clara. It is better to let her
speak for herself. She is a scholar and a teacher as well as a wife
and a mother. Here is her own summing-up, describing how a
teacher is ready to receive as well as to give meaning.

> I learn from Elly and I learn from my students; they also
> teach me about Elly. In the early years, I knew a student who
> was himself emerging from a dark citadel; he had been to the
> Menninger Clinic and to other places too, and he knew from
> inside the ways of thought I had to learn. "Things get too
> much for her and she just turns down the volume," he told me.
> I remembered that, because I have seen it so often since, in Elly
> and in so many others. Human beings fortify themselves in
> many ways. Numbness, weakness, irony, inattention, silence,
> suspicion are only a few of the materials out of which the per-
> sonality constructs its walls. With experience gained in my
> siege of Elly I mount smaller sieges. Each one is undertaken
> with hesitation; to try to help anyone is an arrogance. But Elly
> is there to remind me that to fail to try is a dereliction. Not all
> my sieges are successful. But where I fail, I have learned that
> I fail because of my own clumsiness and inadequacy, not be-
> cause the enterprise is impossible. However formidable the
> fortifications, they can be breached. I have not found one per-
> son, however remote, however hostile, who did not wish for
> what he seemed to fight. Of all the things that Elly has given,
> the most precious is this faith, a faith experience has almost
> transformed into certain knowledge: that inside the strongest
> citadel he can construct, the human being awaits his besieger.

Clara does not need to tell us, because anybody reading her
book knows it already, that outside the first circle of her family
and the second circle of her students there is a third circle, the
circle of her readers, a great multitude of people, teachers, doctors,
parents, friends, and strangers, who all in their different ways can

gather the gift of meaning from her story. And once again the gift works both ways. The book itself gave perspective and illumination and meaning to Clara's private struggle, a struggle which continued for many long years after the book was finished. Clara had always been a natural writer and a lover of literature. She had always believed in the power of written words to redeem the dullness of day-to-day existence. But it was Elly's illness and slow awakening which gave Clara a theme to match her capabilities as a writer. Elly gave Clara the strength of will and the understanding of human suffering which shine through the pages of her book. Through this book Clara reached out and touched the multitude in the third circle. She found herself embarked on a mission like the prophet in Pushkin's poem, who meets an angel at the crossroads and is sent out:

> Over land and sea,
> To burn the hearts of people with a word.

When Elly was twelve years old, I had the impression that she came close to being a totally alien intelligence, such as we might expect to encounter if we were successful in finding an intelligent life-form in some remote part of the galaxy. Astronomers have often asked themselves how we could hope to communicate with an alien intelligence if we were lucky enough to discover one. Perhaps Elly throws a little light on this question. At twelve years old she still had no sense of her own identity. Like many autistic children in the early stages of learning to speak, she used the pronouns "I" and "you" interchangeably. Her mental world must have been radically different from yours and mine. And yet she could communicate quite well with us through the medium of mathematics. While I was staying at her house, a letter arrived for Elly from one of her friends, another autistic child. Elly opened the letter. It contained nothing but a long list of prime numbers. I could see that the numbers were all the primes between one and a thousand. Elly glanced through the list rapidly, then took a pencil and gleefully crossed out the number 703. She was laughing and singing with joy. I asked her why she didn't like the number 703, since it looked to me like a perfectly good prime. She wrote down in large figures so that everyone could see, "$703 = 19 \times 37$." With that there could be no argument. So I knew that even the most alien intelligence has something in common with us. Her prime numbers are the same as ours.

One more public glimpse of Elly was provided by her father, showing her a little later at a crucial stage in her search for meaning. David Park and Philip Youderian published in the *Journal of Autism and Childhood Schizophrenia* an article with the title "Light and Number: Ordering Principles in the World of an Autistic Child." They described a marvelously elaborate and abstract scheme by which Elly at that time attached numbers to her emotions and to the comings and goings of the sun and moon.

> The numbers 73 and 137 are there, carrying their burden of magic, and the concept of the days in general belongs to their product $73 \times 137 = 10001$. What does it all mean? It is not hard to share Elly's meanings to some extent. One may react much as she does to sun and cloud, and see the humor of imagining horrible disasters as long as they cannot possibly happen. Some people respond to the individual qualities of numbers and think it splendid that 70003 is a prime. But these are only fragments of adult thought. For Elly they unite into a harmonious whole, capable of profoundly influencing her mood and her reaction to events. In essence, someone from whom the gift of words has been largely withheld has built a world of light and number . . . . It is clear if one talks with Elly that many of the actions of the people around her, and most of their interests and concerns, have no meaning at all for her. It is our conjecture that Elly's system of ideas represents her effort to fill the deficiency by establishing her own kind of meaning . . . . Elly now talks more than she did when her system was new, though still with great effort and concentration, and she has begun to share with others what she has seen during the day and what has happened at school. Re-

cently, when asked a question about her system, she smiled and said, "I used to care about that last year." Not that it is gone now, but only that there are more and more things to think about now that do not fit into the system.

With these words I will say goodbye to Elly. She has come a long way in the nine years since they were written. It took Elly's parents twenty years to nurture in her a sense of meaning and of human values so that she can now communicate with us as one human being to another. Perhaps in twenty years we can likewise break through our barriers of apathy and denial and face honestly the human implications of our nuclear policies. Elly is now no longer a case-history but a real person, a grown-up person whose privacy needs to be respected. If you want to see for yourselves what she has been doing recently, you can buy one of her paintings, signed with her real name, Jessica Park.

But I have not finished with Clara. Three years ago she published in the *Hudson Review* an article with the title "No Time for Comedy," which speaks more directly than *The Siege* to the concerns of these lectures. I took from her *Hudson Review* article the title and the main message of my talk today. The *Hudson Review* is a writers' magazine, read mostly by people with a professional interest in literature. Clara is saying to her literary colleagues that modern literature in its obsession with gloom and doom has lost touch with reality. She quotes from the Nobel Prize speech of Saul Bellow, my illustrious predecessor as Tanner Lecturer, who stands on her side in this matter: "Essay after essay, book after book . . . maintain . . . the usual things about mass society, dehumanization, and the rest. How weary we are of them. How poorly they represent us. The pictures they offer no more resemble us than we resemble the reconstructed reptiles and other monsters in a museum of paleontology. We are much more limber, versatile, better articulated; there is much more to us; we all feel it."

My message to you is the same. Literature has been, and will be again, the great storehouse of human values. Only at the moment it seems that a large fraction of our writing is dominated by a fashionable cult of meaninglessness. When literature deliberately cultivates meaninglessness, we can hardly look to it as a source of meaning. Literature then becomes, as psychoanalysis was once said to be, the disease of which it is supposed to be the cure. It is no wonder that ordinary people find it irrelevant to the real problems with which they are confronted.

Perhaps a restoration of our spirit may go hand in hand with a restoration of our literature. When we can write truly about ourselves, we shall also be better able to feel truly and act truly. And this brings me back to Clara Park. In *The Siege* she showed what it means to write truly. In the *Hudson Review* article she is saying that the fundamental malaise of our time is a loss of understanding of the ancient art of comedy. Comedy, not in the modern sense of a comedian who tries to be funny on television, but in the ancient sense of comedy as a serious drama ending in a mood of joy rather than sorrow. *The Siege* itself is, in this ancient sense of the word, a comedy. It is a classic drama of courage and love triumphing over obstacles, written in a style and language appropriate to our times.

Let us hear a little of what Clara has to say about tragedy and comedy:

> The Iliad and the Odyssey are the fundamental narratives of Western consciousness, even for those who have not read them: two masks, two modes, two stances; minor chord and major; two primary ways of meeting experience. The Iliad sets the type of tragedy, as Aristotle tells us, where greatness shines amid violence, error, defeat and mortality. The Odyssey celebrates survival among the world's dangers and surprises, and then homecoming, and order restored. It is the very archetype of a prosperous outcome, of Comedy . . . .
>
> Tragedy and Comedy: though the words are paired, their order is not reversible . . . . We can imagine Iliad and Odyssey in only one sequence. To turn back from the long voyage home to the fall of the city, from Odysseus in Penelope's arms to

Hector dead and Achilles' death to come, would be to turn experience upside down . . . . Historically indeed, but above all emotionally, the Odyssey comes last.

Last, as Sophocles at ninety, his proud city collapsing around him, in defeat returned to the bitter legend and brought old Oedipus to the healing grove of Colonus, insisting that though suffering is disproportionate, it is not meaningless but mysteriously confers blessing: last, as Matisse with crippled fingers cut singing color into immense shapes of praise . . . . Shakespeare's sequence makes the same statement; what comes last is not the sovereign Nothing of King Lear but the benign vision of Winter's Tale and The Tempest . . . .

Here on stage stand Ferdinand and Miranda, undertaking once more to live happily ever after, — the young, our own, that simple investment in the future we're all capable of, our built-in second chance. For them the tragic past is only a story that grownups remember. Untendentiously, insouciantly, they will go about their business, the business of comedy, making new beginnings of our bad endings, showing us that they were not endings at all, that there are no endings . . . .

What is at issue today is whether we have grown too conscious and too clever for comedy's burst of good will. In every age but this the creators of our great fictions have regularly accorded us happy endings to stand beside those others that evoke our terror and our pity. Happy endings still exist, of course. But they have lost their ancient legitimacy . . . . They awaken an automatic distrust . . . . And so for the first time since the beginning of our literature there is no major artistic mode to affirm the experience of comedy: healing, restoration, winning through . . . . It is a grand claim we make when we reject happy endings: that we are very special, that whatever songs previous ages could sing, in our terrible century all success is shallow or illusory, all prosperity a fairy-tale; that the only responses to our world which command adult assent are compulsive ironies and cries of pain; that the world which seems to lie before us like a world of dreams, so various, so beautiful, so new, hath, in short, really neither joy nor love nor light, nor certitude, nor peace, nor help for pain, and we are here as on a darkling plain waiting for Godot.

Clara goes on to say that the essential feature of comedy is not the happy ending but the quality of the characters which enables them to earn a happy ending. Odysseus, the prototype of the comic hero, earned his happy ending by being clever, adaptable, devious, opportunistic, and not too much concerned with his own dignity. When it was necessary to escape from a bad situation in the Cyclops' cave, he was willing to take a ride hanging onto the under-belly of a sheep. Here is Homer's image of the human condition, an image which has helped to keep us sane for three thousand years and can still keep us sane if we do not close our eyes to it: the Cyclops stroking the back of his favorite ram, telling it how grievously Odysseus has injured him and asking it where Odysseus has gone, while Odysseus precariously hangs onto the wool underneath, silently hoping for the best. The art of comedy is to make happy endings credible by showing us how they are earned.

"Was Homer's vision," Clara asks, "so much less searching than our own? There is an ugly arrogance in the insistence that our age, alone among all, is too terrible for comedy. In the city of York, in the years when Shakespeare was writing, only ten percent of the population lived to the age of forty. Aristocrats indeed did better; they had nearly an even chance. We cannot imagine what the words 'the shadow of death' meant to our forefathers. The Thirty Years' War left two of every three in Germany dead. Chaucer's pilgrims rode to Canterbury through a countryside which a generation before had been devastated by the Black Death . . . . Any realistic consideration of the life of the past, both in its day-to-day precariousness and its vulnerability to repeated holocaust, will show up our claims to unique misery as uniquely self-centered."

The heroes of comedy are people who do not pity themselves. They take the rough with the smooth. When they are lucky they are not ashamed of it. When they are unlucky they do not despair. Above all, they never give up hope.

There is in the literature of our own century another fine example of tragedy and comedy in action. In December of the

year 1911 the Norwegian explorer Amundsen reached the South
Pole. A month later the British explorer Scott arrived at the Pole.
After heroic exertions, Scott and his companions died in a blizzard
on the way home, only eleven miles from the depot where they
would have found supplies and safety. The story of Scott's expedi-
tion was written ten years later by Apsley Cherry-Garrard in a book
which he called *The Worst Journey in the World*. Cherry-Garrard
was one of the survivors who went out in search of Scott and
found him dead in his tent. Here is his description of the scene.

> Bowers and Wilson were sleeping in their bags. Scott had
> thrown back the flaps of his bag at the end. His left hand was
> stretched out over Wilson, his lifelong friend. Beneath the
> head of his bag, between the bag and the floor-cloth, was the
> green wallet in which he carried his diary . . . .
> We never moved them. We took the bamboos of the tent
> away, and the tent itself covered them. And over them we
> built the cairn.
> I do not know how long we were there, but when all was
> finished and the chapter of Corinthians had been read, it was
> midnight of some day. The sun was dipping low above the
> Pole, the Barrier was almost in shadow. And the sky was blaz-
> ing — sheets and sheets of iridescent clouds. The cairn and
> Cross stood dark against a glory of burnished gold.

Cherry-Garrard ends his last-but-one chapter with the text of
Scott's message to the public, found among the papers in the
tent. After summarizing the causes of the disaster, Scott finishes
on a more personal note: "For four days we have been unable to
leave the tent — the gale howling about us. We are weak, writing is difficult, but for my own sake I do not regret this journey,
which has shown that Englishmen can endure hardships, help one
another, and meet death with as great a fortitude as ever in the
past. We took risks, we knew we took them; things have come out
against us, and therefore we have no cause for complaint, but bow
to the will of Providence, determined still to do our best to the

last . . . . Had we lived, I should have had a tale to tell of the
hardihood, endurance and courage of my companions which would
have stirred the heart of every Englishman. These rough notes and
our dead bodies must tell the tale."

Those are the immortal words of the tragic hero Robert Scott.
But Cherry-Garrard does not stop there. Immediately after those
words he begins a new chapter, his last chapter, with the title
"Never Again." It starts with a quotation from the poet George
Herbert:

And now in age I bud again,
After so many deaths I live and write;
I once more smell the dew and rain,
And relish versing. O my onely light,
It cannot be
That I am he
On whom thy tempests fell all night.

Then Cherry-Garrard goes on:

> I shall inevitably be asked for a word of mature judgment
> of the expedition of a kind that was impossible when we were
> all close up to it, and when I was a subaltern of twenty-four,
> not incapable of judging my elders, but too young to have
> found out whether my judgment was worth anything. I now
> see very plainly that though we achieved a first-rate tragedy,
> which will never be forgotten just because it was a tragedy,
> tragedy was not our business. In the broad perspective opened
> up by ten years' distance, I see not one journey to the pole, but
> two, in startling contrast one to another. On the one hand,
> Amundsen going straight there, getting there first, and return-
> ing without the loss of a single man, and without having put
> any greater strain on himself and his men than was all in the
> day's work of polar exploration. Nothing more businesslike
> could be imagined. On the other hand, our expedition, running
> appalling risks, performing prodigies of superhuman endur-
> ance, achieving immortal renown, commemorated in august
> cathedral sermons and by public statues, yet reaching the Pole
> only to find our terrible journey superfluous, and leaving our

best men dead on the ice. To ignore such a contrast would be
ridiculous; to write a book without accounting for it a waste
of time . . . .

The future explorer . . . will ask, what was the secret of
Amundsen's slick success? What is the moral of our troubles
and losses? I will take Amundsen's success first. Undoubtedly
the very remarkable qualities of the man himself had a good
deal to do with it. There is a sort of sagacity that constitutes
the specific genius of the explorer: and Amundsen proved his
possession of this by his guess that there was terra firma in the
Bay of Whales as solid as on Ross Island. Then there is the
quality of big leadership which is shown by daring to take a
big chance. Amundsen took a very big one indeed when he
turned from the route to the Pole explored and ascertained by
Scott and Shackleton and determined to find a second pass over
the mountains from the Barrier to the plateau. As it happened,
he succeeded, and established his route as the best way to the
Pole until a better is discovered. But he might easily have
failed and perished in the attempt; and the combination of reasoning and daring that nerved him to make it can hardly be
overrated. All these things helped him. Yet any rather con-
servative whaling captain might have refused to make Scott's
experiment with motor transport, ponies and man-hauling, and
stuck to the dogs; and it was this quite commonplace choice
that sent Amundsen so gaily to the Pole and back, with no
abnormal strain on men or dogs, and no great hardship either.
He never pulled a mile from start to finish.

This is as much as I have time for of Cherry-Garrard's post-
mortem examination. You can find another glimpse of Amundsen
in John McPhee's recent book *Coming into the Country*.* McPhee's
book is about Alaska. He describes how on a wintry day in 1905,
with the temperature at sixty below, Amundsen quietly and un-
obtrusively walked into the post office at Eagle, Alaska, to send a
telegram home to Norway announcing that he had completed
the first crossing of the Northwest Passage. The last four hundred

* New York: Farrar, Straus and Giroux, 1977.

miles he had traveled alone with his sled and dog-team. No fuss, no cathedral sermons. That was six years before he arrived at the South Pole.

Cherry-Garrard's final verdict on the two South Pole expeditions was simple. "There is a sort of sagacity that constitutes the specific genius of the explorer." Amundsen had it. Scott didn't. The word "sagacity" is carefully chosen. Sagacity is not the same thing as wisdom. Wisdom is the greater virtue, but it is too rare and too solemn for everyday use. Sagacity is by comparison rather cheap, rather slick, rather undignified, but nine times out of ten it is sagacity that will get you out quicker when you are stuck in a bad hole. The shipwrecked mariner in Kipling's Just-So story "How the Whale Got His Throat" was "a man of infinite resource and sagacity," and so he naturally knew how to trick the whale into giving him a free ride back to England. Three thousand years earlier, Odysseus showed the same sort of sagacity in dealing with the Cyclops. Sagacity is the essential virtue for the hero of a comedy. It is the art of making the best of a bad job, the art of finding the practical rather than the ideal solution to a problem, the art of lucking out when things look hopeless.

Cherry-Garrard gives Scott his due. It was true, as Cherry-Garrard says, that Scott's life and death made a first-rate tragedy. First-rate in every sense, in the nobility of character of the hero, in the grandeur of the geographical setting, in the epic quality of Scott's prose, and in the tragic flaw of Scott's nature, the pride and stubbornness which led him to demand more of himself and of his companions than was humanly possible. A first-rate tragedy indeed, worthy of all the fine speeches and sermons that have been devoted to it. And yet, Cherry-Garrard, who lived through it, has the last word. Tragedy, he says, was not our business. When all is said and done, Amundsen knew his business as an explorer and Scott didn't. The business of an explorer is not tragedy but survival.

The main thing I am trying to say in this talk is that Cherry-Garrard's words apply to us too. Tragedy is not our business.

Too much preoccupation with tragedy is bad for our mental health. Tragedy is a real and important part of the human condition, but it is not the whole of it. Some people try to make a tragedy out of every aspect of modern life. In the end their mental state comes to resemble the attitude of another famous character of modern fiction:

> Eeyore, the old grey Donkey, stood by the side of the stream, and looked at himself in the water.
> "Pathetic," he said. "That's what it is. Pathetic."
> He turned and walked slowly down the stream for twenty yards, splashed across it, and walked slowly back on the other side. Then he looked at himself in the water again.
> "As I thought," he said. "No better from this side. But nobody minds. Nobody cares. Pathetic, that's what it is." *

The Eeyore syndrome is somewhere deep in the heart of each one of us, ready to take over if we give it a chance. Anyone who has to deal with mentally sick people will be familiar with the voice of Eeyore. Those of us who consider ourselves sane often feel like that too. The best antidote that we have against the Eeyore syndrome is comedy, comedy in the new-fashioned sense, making fun of ourselves, and also comedy in the old-fashioned sense, the drama of people like Odysseus and Amundsen who survive by using their wits. Survival is our business, and in that business it is the heroes of comedy who have the most to teach us.

Odysseus and his friends can teach us a trick or two which may come in handy when we are in a tight spot. But the tricks are not important. The important thing which comedy does for us is to show us meanings. Just as the central theme of the *Iliad* is death, the central theme of the *Odyssey* is homecoming. The homecoming of Odysseus gives meaning to his adventures and his sufferings. Homecoming is still in the modern world a powerful symbol and a source of meaning. Millions of Americans come home each year

---

* A. A. Milne, *Winnie-the-Pooh* (New York: E. P. Dutton and Co., 1926), p. 70.

for Thanksgiving. The homecoming of Jews to Jerusalem gave meaning to their two-thousand-year Odyssey.

Homecoming is the reward for survival, but it is not the end of the story. There is no end, because homecoming means a new beginning. Homecoming means renewal and rebirth, a new generation growing up with new hopes and new ideals. Their achievements will redeem our failures; their survival will give meaning to our bewilderment. This is the lesson of comedy. No matter how drastically the institution of the family is changed, no matter how authoritatively it is declared moribund, the family remains central to our social and mental health. The children find meaning by searching for their roots; the parents find meaning by watching their children grow.

Clara Park's book *The Siege* is a celebration of the remedial power of the family. It is family love and discipline which breaks through the isolation of a sick child and gives meaning to the suffering of the parents. William Bradford's book *Of Plymouth Plantation* is also, in the same classic tradition, a comedy, and it is altogether appropriate that it ends with a family chronicle, a list of the surviving Pilgrims and their descendants unto the third and fourth generations:

> Of these hundred persons which came first over in this first ship together, the greater half died in the general mortality, and most of them in two or three months' time. And for those which survived, though some were ancient and past procreation, and others left the place and country, yet of those few remaining are sprung up above 160 persons in this thirty years, and are now living in this present year 1650, besides many of their children which are dead and come not within this account. And of the old stock, of one and other, there are yet living this present year, 1650, near thirty persons. Let the Lord have the praise, who is the High Preserver of men.

Many of us do not share Bradford's religious belief, but we can all share his pride and his hope. Pride for what the old people have done, hope for what the young people will do. The most important lesson which comedy has to teach us is never to give up hope.

This lesson, not to give up hope, is the essential lesson for people to learn who are trying to save the world from nuclear destruction. There are no compelling technical or political reasons why we and the Russians, and even the French and the Chinese too, should not in time succeed in negotiating our nuclear weapons all the way down to zero. The obstacles are primarily institutional and psychological. Too few of us believe that negotiating down to zero is possible. To achieve this goal, we shall need a worldwide awakening of moral indignation pushing the governments and their military establishments to get rid of these weapons which in the long run endanger everybody and protect nobody. We shall not be finished with nuclear weapons in a year or in a decade. But we might, if we are lucky, be finished with them in a half-century, or in about the same length of time that it took the abolitionists to rid the world of slavery. We should not worry too much about the technical details of weapons and delivery systems. The basic issue before us is very simple. Are we, or are we not, ready to face the uncertainties of a world in which nuclear weapons have been negotiated all the way down to zero? If the answer to this question is yes, then there is hope for us and for our grandchildren. And here I will let Clara Park have the last word: "Hope is not the lucky gift of circumstance or disposition, but a virtue like faith and love, to be practiced whether or not we find it easy or even natural, because it is necessary to our survival as human beings."

Arms Control and Peace Research

RAYMOND ARON

THE TANNER LECTURES ON HUMAN VALUES

Delivered at
Clare Hall, Cambridge University

November 22, 1979

RAYMOND ARON studied philosophy at the Ecole Normale Supérieure and at the Sorbonne. Following the *agrégation de philosophie*, he studied in Germany, especially the phenomenologists Husserl and Heidegger and the sociologists, primarily Max Weber. Before the war, he published books on German sociology and philosophy of history and an *Introduction to the Philosophy of History*. After the war, he combined a journalistic career as columnist for *Figaro*, from 1947 to 1977, and now the *Express*, with teaching at the Sorbonne and finally at the Collège de France. His best-known books are *The Opium of the Intellectuals*, *Eighteen Lectures on Industrial Society*, *Peace and War among Nations*, *Essay on Liberties*, *Penser la guerre*, *Clausewitz*, and *In Defense of Decadent Europe*.

The juxtaposition of the two notions *arms control* and *peace research* may at first sight surprise the reader. The first notion implies theoretical and practical research into the ways first, of reducing the risk of war, and nuclear war in particular; second, of reducing devastation if in spite of everything war were to break out; and third, of reducing the cost of armaments and slowing down the arms race. The second notion encompasses all studies relating to the causes of wars and, in more general terms, all the situations and practices dangerous to peace.

The classical period of arms control, a conception of American origin, occurred during the later 1950's and the early 1960's. It developed in response to the strategic and technical studies carried out on nuclear arms and their impact on diplomacy and war. The peace research institutes which proliferated mainly during the 1960's were often in opposition to the American institutes, which concentrated chiefly on nuclear weapons and strategy. The research centres which use the word 'peace' in their titles do not limit their focus to the two European blocs, to American and Soviet strategy, or to nuclear weapons. The inequality among nations and the world economic order also come under their scrutiny insofar as they are causes of conflict, and at any event manifestations of violence — 'structural violence', as the adherents of this school choose to call it.

In other words, arms control specialists tend to be primarily interested in nuclear weapons and the dangers of war related to them. Peace research specialists, on the other hand, tend to broaden out their investigations to cover all forms of armaments and violence. Of the two schools, only the first has exercised any influence on statesmen and the course of events. Some of the ideas thrown out by academics and think-tank researchers have been taken up and put into practice. The SALT I and SALT II agreements, for example, spring from the school of arms control. And the debate provoked by SALT II raises questions concerning the basis of arms control itself.

*   *   *

The French term *maîtrise des armements* conveys the original intention of *arms control* rather better than the English expression. Arms control implies neither disarmament, verification, nor inspection, but a refusal to give in to the dynamic of the arms race. It implies the will to become again, as Descartes put it, both master and possessor of nature — or in this case, arms. Disarmament is not necessarily the aim, since its chief objective is to prevent war, and it has not been established that disarmament invariably helps to prevent it. For example, in retrospect, most people would admit that, faced with Hitler in 1935, rearmament would have been preferable to disarmament. The theoreticians of arms control do not adopt the thesis that wars are a result of the arms race. They study the means by which, in a given situation, the risk of war can be prevented from increasing through either an excess or an insufficiency of arms. The balance of terror is better safeguarded by a few hundred rather than by a few dozen intercontinental missiles.

The theory of arms control, almost self-evident in its principles, would not have been of any special interest in itself if the conjunction of superpower rivalry and the existence of nuclear weapons had not presented what might be a perfect example of 'arms control'. The supporters of this theory take as a starting point that a genuine and fundamental political consensus between the United States and the Soviet Union is out of the question. They also hold that both rivals hope to avoid a nuclear conflict. Starting from these two premises, arms control consists in fixing the relationship of force between the two superpowers at a level compatible with both the *desire of each side to get the better of the other in confrontations if possible*, and their *common desire* not to destroy each other. The stumbling block, and perhaps the contradiction, inherent in this theory lies in the clash between the *obviously antagonistic goals* of the two powers and their *assumed common interest.* Is it really possible to agree on a limitation of armaments favorable to the nonuse of nuclear weapons without, on another level, political or military, favouring one or other of the protagonists?

The first steps in arms control were expressions of *the common purpose*, which, by their nature, did not excite much controversy. The best example is the telephone hot line. It is important, in the heat of a crisis, that the two heads of state be able to communicate directly. Dialogue is not enough to guarantee a solution, but it offers a better chance for avoiding the worst. A second agreement attributable to arms control is the partial suspension of nuclear tests. Common human interest justifies the ban on tests within the atmosphere, so as not to pollute the air we breathe and to avoid radioactive fallout from which other populations would suffer. The comprehensive test ban would slow down or prevent the deployment of new or better weapons.

But the ban has also served another purpose of arms control: to hinder what is called the proliferation (or dissemination) of nuclear weapons and the enlargement of the atomic club. I don't propose to analyse the basis of this theory in detail here: I would simply like to make the point that the ban does embody certain political implications. The first powers to employ nuclear weapons are attempting to reserve this weapon, monstrous or decisive, for themselves — which invites the question, from a preoccupation with peace in general or from self-interest?

Other measures — the renunciation of chemical and biological weapons, and the nonmilitarisation of space and ocean bed — caused no stir. The agreement regarding the nonmilitarisation of space has been partially respected so far: no bombs have been put in space (it has not presented any apparent military advantage).

But it is widely known that the Soviets have carried out experiments in the destruction of satellites and that the Americans, in turn, are working on similar projects.

* * *

The first arms limitation agreement was signed by Leonid Brezhnev and Richard Nixon in 1972, together with a declaration laying down the mode of conduct to which the two signatories subscribed. The two signing states committed themselves to restraint (the favorite word of the Secretary of State at the time). They would not try to take 'unilateral advantage' at each other's expense. The link between arms limitation and the diplomatic conduct of the two superstates did not bring about a visible change either in Moscow or in Washington. The same mixture of limited cooperation and permanent opposition still marks their intercourse. (The two superpowers, according to the theory, agree on the ceiling of strategic nuclear arms imposed on each of them in the hope of slowing down the arms race in this field and creating a stable situation that should reduce the risk of war and the actual use of these weapons.)

This treaty and a second, which has still not been ratified by the Senate, have only done away with or, rather, impeded the development of a single system of weapons: antiballistic missiles, or what the Americans call ABM. The Soviets had already installed an ABM system around Moscow which, according to the Americans, was of doubtful efficiency. Meanwhile, the Americans were in the process of setting up their own system which the military leaders hoped to deploy at least around Washington and to protect the silos of intercontinental missiles. According to Henry Kissinger, when Lyndon Johnson brought up the question of a common abandonment of ABM, Premier Kosygin replied that he had never heard such a stupid proposal. But a few months later the Soviets were eagerly underwriting that very proposal: the conscious and determined decision to give up all defence against missiles, or, in other words, to *guarantee the vulnerability* of the territory of the two superpowers. Each of the two reserved the right to protect one site. The United States, at least, has not used that right.

The abandonment of ABM, whatever its accidental cause, had one lasting significance in that it revealed the inspiration behind arms control. What was the objective of the SALT negotiators? Stability: another word for equilibrium but with its own connotation. According to press commentators, the relationship between the two great nuclear powers would be stable on the day when neither of the two would be tempted to have recourse to these weapons, knowing that the reprisals would be equally destructive to themselves. This assurance of reciprocal destruction is reinforced by the *absence of defence* and by the *vulnerability of the cities*, but, at the same time, by the *invulnerability of the weapons of retaliation*. From here one passes from stability to the idea of *mutually assured destruction*, also known as MAD. Nuclear weapons, according to this doctrine, have no other function than to prevent their own military use.

The writers of the *New York Times*, for example, argued against the technology of the MIRV's (multiple independently-targetable re-entry vehicles). To the Soviets, the massive increase in the number of nuclear warheads would constitute a threat because it reinforced American counterforce capability. Without any doubt, the Soviets would go on to do the same, increasing the number of their launchers or their warheads. Either one of the two would ensure a substantive superiority for itself and put the opposing forces in danger; according to this hypothesis, stability would be compromised. Another possibility, far more probable, would be that the two camps would regain the same stability and the same strike capability, but on a higher level of both expenditure and number of weapons. Events confirmed the second alternative. But the academic strategists had never accepted such a simplistic interpretation of deterrence during the 1960's.

If it is demanded of the nuclear force of the United States only that it should be able to inflict enormous devastation on the aggressor at a second strike, the task of those in power is singularly simplified. The 41 submarines, each carrying 16 MIRV'ed missiles, alone can inflict untold damage on the Soviet Union (and not even that number is necessary). However, such an action against enemy resources would be more or less suicidal, because it would call down upon American cities an equivalent catastrophe.

In other words, the theory of arms control, in this form, implies a strategic doctrine. If one defines stability as the invulnerability of the main forces of the two superpowers, arms control should aim not only at stability, but at the elimination of all counterforce capability. For the counterforce capability of one camp presupposes the vulnerability, if only partial, of the enemy force. This explains why some statesmen of the United States, Robert MacNamara in particular, seemed both to want and to fear the counterforce capability that they still possessed by the early 1960's. MacNamara repeatedly advised the Soviets to protect their missiles better and to reinforce their silos. His reasoning was that the Soviets would be tempted to strike first if they thought they were at the mercy of an American first strike.

Via these arguments, arms control leads to what the strategists call the *minimum deterrent*, the capacity to deter the adversary from a nuclear attack against one's own territory. But with or without arms control both the United States and the Soviet Union already wield this minimal deterring power. Years of negotiation would not have been necessary to arrive at this kind of stability — a partial stability, limited to a single level of strategic nuclear weaponry. Is this kind of partial stability in conformity with the strategic doctrine of American diplomacy? Is the minimum deterrent sufficient to guarantee the security of the allies of the United States? Stability at one level, restricted to one type of weaponry, does not, by itself, stabilise the overall relations between the two superstates.

* * *

Beyond the abandonment of ABM, SALT I fixed a ceiling on the number of intercontinental missiles the two superpowers were allowed to own. The Soviets were allotted a ceiling around 40 percent higher than the Americans, who, thanks to MIRV technology, owned a far higher number of nuclear warheads. The Senate ratified SALT I without much resistance. It did, however, demand that the subsequent treaty should re-establish equality in the number of the two superpowers' intercontinental missiles.

The intercontinental ballistic missile systems of the United States and the Soviet Union present such structural differences that trying to determine equality or parity or equivalence leads to endless discussion. The negotiators finally agreed on the total number of strategic nuclear missiles (2,400 and subsequently — from January 1, 1982—2,250), the total number of land-launched missiles equipped with MIRV's (820), the total number of MIRV'ed missiles (1,320), and the maximum number of nuclear warheads inserted in a single heavy missile (10).

In SALT I, there was one ceiling for land-based missiles, another for SLBM's. In SALT II, there remains a ceiling for all intercontinental missiles, but inside this total global number of launchers each one of the two signatories retains the right to determine the composition of the aggregates, the percentages of ICBM's, SLBM's, and bombers. On the Soviet side, the proportion of ICBM's is 62 percent, on the American side only 40 percent. SALT II attempts to slow down, if not to stop altogether, the renewal of arms and quantitative progress by specific measures. The original internal volume of an ICBM silo launcher should not be increased by more than 32 percent; there is the interdiction against increasing the launch-weight or the throw-weight of the heavy ICBM, flight testing or deploying new types of ICBM's (with the exception of one light model), the interdiction against increasing the number of reentry vehicles for the ICBM, SLBM, etc.

There is still today a passionate debate about SALT II, advantages and dangers. It is not my purpose to go into the details of the controversy in order to discuss the consequences of the treaty for Europe. I shall concentrate on the key objections of the adversaries of the treaty, leaving aside also the uncertainties of verification.

The Soviet heavy launcher, the SS-18, can carry up to ten nuclear warheads. The ceiling on the SS-18 is fixed at 308. If the nuclear warheads of these heavy launchers have the firing accuracy that the Americans think they do, they could destroy at a single blow almost the entire United States force of Minutemen, other land-launched missiles, and airfields. These are the most accurate missiles, the best adapted to counterforce. In response to a hypothetical destruction of the American land-launched missiles, the President of the United States could only use either the submarine-launched missiles or the bombers, equipped with cruise missiles or not, at the risk of triggering mutual destruction, the devastation of the industrial system, and a senseless orgy of violence.

SALT II's supporters do not deny that towards 1983 the Soviets will indeed have the capacity to destroy some 90 percent of the United States' land-launched missiles, whereas under the treaty the United States would not have the equivalent capacity to destroy the Soviet land-launched missiles. As of June 12, 1979, the United States had at its disposal, in addition to 1,054 land-launched missiles, 656 submarine-launched missiles (including 496 equipped with MIRV's), and 573 heavy bombers. Whatever the effectiveness of a Soviet first strike, it could not take away from the United States its capacity for massive reprisals. But having once destroyed the American land-launched missiles in a first strike, the Soviet Union would still have more than enough missiles to lay waste the territory of the United States.

In theory, this sort of stability at the level of strategic nuclear weaponry should weaken the deterrent effect of these weapons in relation to all acts of aggression, with the exception of the most serious of all those directed at the vital interests of the country and the integrity of its territory. In other words, the desired effect of the doctrine of mutually assured destruction is in the direction of a neutralisation of these weapons. And, at the same time, conflicts at a lower level, even armed ones, become less improbable.

Furthermore, has this so-called stability really been established at the level of intercontinental missiles? Is the unequal vulnerability of the Soviet and American land-launched missiles really compatible with stability? Once again, according to all the experts, whether for or against SALT II, the Soviets, with their heavy missiles, will in two or three years' time have the capacity to eliminate the system of American land-launched missiles at a first strike, whereas the Americans will not be able to do the same. In other words, the Soviets are supposed to have a first strike capacity superior to that of the Americans. Does this superiority have serious implications? Most people will hesitate here: the very idea of such a war is so repellent, the scenario so improbable, that it is difficult to take these macabre calculations entirely seriously. If one enters into these analyses, Soviet superiority depends on the inaccuracy of the SLBM. The next SLBM, the Trident, could be just as accurate as the ICBM and be fired at the remaining Soviet land-based launchers without aiming at the cities. (Even during the time of planned massive retaliation, the Americans did not target on the cities, but at military or economic objectives. Still, the collateral destruction would have been, and, in spite of improved firing accuracy, would still today be enormous.) Soviet superiority consists in launching-weight and throw-weight, the megatonnage which improves the counterforce capability.

What effect does the uncertain stability of the intercontinental nuclear forces have on the relationship between the two superpowers? Here also the reply is far from clear cut. Nuclear weapons cannot fail to have an influence on those in power, on both sides, encouraging them to be prudent. But Henry Kissinger himself has gone back on the remark he made once to journalists during an interview: "In the name of God, what does superiority mean in this field?" Should genuine equality at the level of intercontinental weapons be established, the relative force in other areas, and in Europe in particular, takes on an increased significance. The West can no longer count on the threat of escalation. Nor can it count on its superiority on a higher level to compensate for its inferiority at the lower levels. Put more explicitly, it can neither count on tactical nuclear weapons to weigh against its inadequate number of divisions nor make up for the number of Soviet medium-range missiles through the number of its intercontinental missiles. For Europe, 'theatre' weaponry thus becomes an essential element of security.

The Americans have proposed what is in effect a prolongation of SALT I into SALT II, which will deal with so-called 'gray areas'. Without discussing the problem at length, I shall express my skepticism. The negotiations of SALT I and SALT II neither modified the programmes of the two signatories nor prevented the development of the offensive missiles the Soviet Union wanted to produce. By limiting the enlargement of launching silo volume, the American negotiators hoped to avoid the mass production of heavy missiles. They failed; the Soviet experts were able to insert heavy missiles into their launching silos without enlarging them. In the negotiations concerning Europe, what could the American–Europeans trade off against the tanks, the guns, the planes, the SS-20's of Soviet weaponry? Quantitatively, the Soviet side is superior in all fields. On what basis would stability be founded?

Beyond that, during the SALT negotiations discussion had already been complicated by distinctions made between the various types as well as numbers of missiles. As a result of the heterogeneous natures of the two different systems, the notion of equality has been brought into question. And furthermore, inequality in first-strike capacity has finally been agreed upon, deriving from the technical and perhaps strategic choices of the two parties. In any negotiation on theatre weapons, it would be difficult to ignore the basic differences in the two sides' approach to strategy. NATO, a fragile coalition of democratic governments, is by nature incapable of taking initiatives. If war does break out in Europe, the offensive will necessarily come from the East. And in so narrow a theatre of operations, the offensive takes on a decisive importance, as shown by the wars in the Middle East. How important is the number of planes and even of tactical nuclear weapons if the nuclear warheads of the SS-20's can, at a blow, destroy a few hundred points crucial to the defence of the West?

The doctrine of arms control assumed a common wish on the part of the two great superpowers not to destroy each other — that they would not use nuclear weapons against each other. But, in the case of Europe, Soviet military treatises anticipate a lightning strike, with the simultaneous deployment of both conventional and nuclear weapons. The West does not know which kind of war it should be preparing for.

I arrive here at a conclusion that you will perhaps find too categorical: that the doctrine of arms control has been a failure so far.

1. First of all, it has not helped to reduce military expenditure, or even caused a reduction in the sums spent on nuclear weapons. The ceilings laid down leave margins for both the production of new launchers and their improvement. Since SALT I, the Soviets have deployed many new systems: ICBM, SS-16, -18, -19, SS.N.18 SLBM; the Americans have MIRV'ed their Minutemen II and III and Poseidon. Jimmy Carter had promised to produce 200 MX and the Trident after the ratification of SALT II. Ronald Reagan will probably do more.

2. The negotiators have been overtaken by the speed of technical progress. Counting launchers is a crude yardstick; the

diversity of missiles and their possibilities, the differences in strategic attitudes make stability a more complex matter than simply counting the number of weapons.

3. The Americans took as a starting point the hypothesis of a common desire on the part of the superpowers not to destroy each other. This hypothesis is indeed a highly probable one. But there are two ways of achieving the aim of avoiding war: parity or superiority. The Americans originally bet on superiority, and it may be that the Soviets are now wagering on superiority in turn. In their treatises, the Soviet strategists refute the Western theory that neither camp can win a nuclear war. They maintain that even nuclear war would not be an exception to Clausewitz's maxim that war is the continuation of state policy by other means. Nuclear war, they affirm, which could be avoided, would, if it were to break out, mark the final episode in the struggle between the two socioeconomic formations, socialism and capitalism. Do they really believe it? No one knows.

4. Even supposing that an approximate parity were to be established at the level of intercontinental missiles, the relative neutralization of those arms would not necessarily entail the same consequences for both camps. Everything would depend on the relative forces at lower levels and in other theatres of operation.

Some members of the arms control community will object that the arms race would have been worse without SALT. It is true that ABM has been prevented, but is this an achievement or a cardinal error? The idea was to stop first the defensive and then the offensive arms. The increase of offensive arms, the heavy missiles, numbers of warheads, continued. It is true that SALT II limits the freedom of the two sides on certain points, for example the mobile missiles. But, here again, with an exception: the Soviets have already produced, tested, and deployed the SS-20, an intermediate-range missile which threatens the entire NATO defense system. The cost of MX will be increased because mobile launchers have been excluded by SALT II (in order to make verification possible). Even without ratification of SALT II, the new administration will avoid systems which would make verification impossible.

Should we, in the opposite direction, place the responsibility for the degradation of the balance of power between the superpowers on arms control? I do not think so. At least, the responsibility of arms control is a limited one. In any event, the Soviet Union possessed the means necessary to reach some sort of parity with the United States: the financial resources, technicians, and industry. The leaders of the Communist party do not stint when it comes to armaments: neither money nor the best brains are spared in the pursuit of military absolutes. It may be that their obsession with arms control causes the American leaders to forget the balance of power and remain passive in the face of the Soviet accumulation of armament.

Henry Kissinger said recently that "rarely, in history, has a nation accepted so passively such a radical change in the military balance. It is not the consequence of SALT, it is the consequence of unilateral decisions extended over a decade and a half, of a strategic doctrine adopted during the sixties, of the bitter domestic divisions growing out of the war in Vietnam, and of the choices made by the present administration . . . ." The doctrine of arms control did not dictate the clauses of SALT I, any more than it did the attitude adopted by the United States between 1973 and 1978, when the extent of Soviet military strength and the deployment of the SS-16, -18, -19, and -20 came to light. The leaders of the United States judged their nuclear force sufficient to remain an efficient deterrent. But as the negotiations drew to a close, the senators could not fail to appreciate the modification of the balance of power.

Arms control had assisted in the decline of American power and helped to conceal it. SALT II, all in all, enshrines and ratifies the decisions taken unilaterally by the two sides. The Soviet Union has spent and manufactured more. The United States has contented itself with the land-launched MIRV'ed missiles of the 1960's and adhered to the 'triad' theory: the capacity for massive reprisals on a second strike and a reduced counterforce. The American strategists assumed that the first strike would come from the East, and in order to assure the invulnerability of the missiles put the majority of them to sea. The Soviets were not afraid to suffer a first strike.

*   *   *

Arms control is inspired by a doctrine and defines its goals. The peace research institutes are of an altogether different nature. That is why the following observations on these institutes are of quite a different nature from those that I have developed in the preceding pages. The directives issuing from arms control, which are, in a certain sense, operational, are open to criticism because they have observable results which bring its very principles into question. Peace research, which is purely academic in essence, does not lead to any practical application, unless one considers it borne out by general propositions, which are always open to contestation.

The literature on peace and war is immense and has grown even faster since the last war. A plethora of different disciplines has been put to the test. Historians, sociologists, economists, psychologists, and psychiatrists have pooled their efforts. But the fact remains that we don't know much more than we did before. We have no basis from which to deduce principles for action.

Take one example: armament or the arms race. Are we in any position to state that the arms race necessarily ends in war? As long as one defines the term in a sufficiently broad and vague way, one could say that the great wars of modern times have been preceded by arms races. But whether the states increased their military budgets because they were preparing for war or whether war was brought on by the accumulation of arms is another matter. In the case of neither world war is the answer straightforward.

As to the war of 1939, the most plausible reply is that the rearmament of the Third Reich was determined by Hitler's diplomatic projects. The West was slow to respond, but in the end did rearm, fearing the Führer's ambition.

The military budgets of the great European nations increased in the years immediately preceding 1914, during what is called the 'armed peace'. But these budgets remained relatively small in terms of gross national product. They did not weigh insupportably upon the finances of the different states or upon the standard of living of the populations. Diplomatic tensions raised fears of an armed conflict and politicians took precautions. France's 'loi de trois ans', the subject of furious polemic, was intended to diminish the inferiority of the French army in relation to that of the Germans, despite the difference in numbers between their two populations.

One can speak of an arms race today, but not without certain reservations. The United States devotes 5 percent of its GNP to the national defence budget. In western Europe the percentage hovers around 3.5. Estimates for the Soviet Union vary between 11 and 15 percent, equivalent, in percentage terms, to two or three times that of the United States. In absolute terms, military expenditure is considerable — more than $100 billion in the United States. This expenditure arouses the imagination and also the indignation of people of good will who weigh the value in real wealth — food, education, industry, and health — that the money could be spent on rather than missiles, submarines, and tanks. But this expenditure does not crush whole peoples or give vogue to the sentiment that it would be better to have done with it all rather than endure this endless terror.

Leaving aside the futile questions: who is responsible? and who began it all? we should remember two facts, peculiar to their era, which contribute to the so-called qualitative arms race. Like all industrial products, arms can be improved. Because of this, all states feel more or less obliged to renew the machines of war, obsolescent rather than worn out, before they have even used them. The SS-18 outclasses the Minuteman III. In countless ways the struggle between the armour and the sword continues on land and sea, in air and space.

A second historical fact explains the arms race today: the strategic groundplan that emerged from the last war. On one hand, the intercontinental missiles face each other over oceans and peoples; and on the other hand, the Soviet army, equipped for the offensive, is stationed right in the heart of Europe. This state of affairs makes it probable that in time of war there would be no time to mobilize. The decisive battle would be waged with active, not potential, forces. Even more than before 1914, the military consider the first battles to be decisive. The trend towards professional armies is partially explained by the conception of a probable war.

Peace research institutes more often than not deplore the wastage of resources devoted to armaments. But they haven't, to my knowledge, found either an original method of disarmament or an unknown cause for the arms race. Nor have they proved that the states which arm themselves the most, the Soviet Union and the United States, are dragged by their defence budgets towards an inevitable war.

Let us move on from the explanation of wars by the arms race to a theory which still carries weight in certain circles: that capitalism becomes imperialism and that this, in turn, provokes war. By definition, it runs, the capitalist countries are unable to agree upon the division of the planet and are animated by insatiable greed. But whatever the relationship between the so-called capitalist economy and war, experience does not in any way allow us to imagine that war will disappear with capitalism. The tension between the Soviet Union and the People's Republic of China, and between Vietnam and Cambodia, at the very least suggests the general proposition that ethnic rivalries and historical conflicts survive revolutions and remain equally alive even when govern-

ments profess the same ideology. Furthermore, the great wars of
the century set against one another nations which belonged to the
centre of the world market. It was they who had the most to fear
and the least to hope for from struggles which pushed them to the
extremes of their available resources.

Certain of the peace institutes have brought into vogue a particular representation of the capitalist world: at the centre the
industrialised or wealthy nations, and on the periphery the nations
of the third world, from which the states of the world obtain the
raw materials necessary for their industries, and part of their
surplus value, through the intermediary of the multinational companies. This distinction between the centre and the periphery is
reproduced within each state. The centre of the central states
levies the surplus value from its own internal periphery and leaves
a part to it. In the same way the centre of the peripheral states
profits from a share of the surplus value it takes from its internal
periphery, while pleading integration in the world market —
often to its own interest.

This interpretation does not seem to me to make an important
contribution to the comprehension of war and peace. It helps to
explain national wars of liberation, although the desire for liberation, in the sense of rejecting a foreign colonial power, is also
fuelled by elemental sentiments. At any rate, in the twentieth
century it is the war between the states of the centre which has
devastated the planet: the claim that it is no more than a quarrel
over booty is far from convincing. Since 1945, Japan and West
Germany have proved that they did not need conquest to prosper,
and that they could take for themselves a large part of the external
surplus value without reducing the other central states to slavery.

The distinction between the centre and the periphery suggests a
representation of the world of the states comparable to the Marxist
representation of every collectivity. A minority of exploiters
appropriates the surplus value, taken directly from the workers.
In the states of periphery, a double exploitation is working at the

expense of the workers: the centre exploits its own periphery and lets the world centre exploit the entire peripheral collectivity. The privileged classes by definition take for themselves a part of the profits that agricultural and industrial enterprises have engendered. The multinational companies, insofar as they transfer their profits, cream off the periphery's surplus value to spend or invest elsewhere. Viewed from a neoclassical standpoint, the same facts would appear in a new light, with one main difference: are the profits of foreign investors always the fruit of exploitation? Are they always contrary to the interest of the developing country? Do the prices at which the industrialised states buy primary products from the peripheral states really represent a form of exploitation? It is not possible, in the context of a conference, to analyse the concept of exploitation, object of controversy between the neoclassical and Marxian schools. I will only make the problem explicit.

Before 1973 the price of oil stood at a level that is commonly thought of today as unjustified, despite the fact that the cost of extraction in Saudi Arabia was and is extremely low. Today, operating like a cartel, the producers can fix prices and manipulate production so that an on-the-spot market rise at Rotterdam can cause an increase in prices fixed on contract.

And if one considers market prices as a norm, the argument is the same: regarding raw materials, there is nothing to stop one of the producers from cutting back production or one of the consumers from abruptly releasing available stocks onto the market. Brazil, for example, acting despite the number of other producers, now knows how to manipulate the coffee market legally, without a cartel, by controlling the supply in order to control prices.

Such research, which has only a remote or indirect connection with peace, plays an important part in the studies of some peace research institutes. Whether or not the structure of the capitalist world market is unjust, it has not determined the great wars. It has perhaps accelerated the revolt of the colonised countries, and it probably fuels diplomatic and commercial disputes between the governments of the third world and the wealthy nations. But it was not the source of the two great wars of the century, and it is not at the root of the rivalry between the two great powers, between Vietnam and Cambodia, between India and Pakistan.

The peace institutes, it must be admitted, are often anxious to single out or to define a real peace, as distinct from an 'absence of war'. In his treatise on politics, Spinoza made the distinction. Peace should be more than an absence of war. In the field of international relations, peace is often not more than the absence of war. The peace treaty imposed by the victorious state is tolerated by the defeated because of the lack of force to change it. There are many instances where the peace treaty is only an armistice. Regarding the so-called economic order, it is today commonly affirmed that it is unjust and imposed by the centre upon the periphery. From this view one deduces the concept of 'structural violence'; the world market appears as a manifestation of violence, more or less the equivalent of war.

This kind of analysis errs in the opposite direction from that of the arms control specialists who concentrate on a particular type of weapon, as if the nonutilisation of intercontinental missiles were the same as the nonutilisation of all kinds of arms. Those analysts who see structural violence in the world market imagine that in combating that kind of violence they are working for peace. Both parties are deceiving themselves: the theoreticians of arms control because they isolate a single kind of arms, and the peace research specialists because they extend the concept of war indefinitely.

The partisans of arms control start from an idea which is in fact justified: that nuclear weapons possess such a potential for destruction that it is not unreasonable to attempt to prevent their use, while resigning ourselves to non-nuclear wars. Some specialists in peace research start from the false premise that peace requires justice. In fact, peace has been imposed when and where an imperial power has dictated it or when enemies, exhausted by their fighting, have either found a way to reconciliation or perceived the threat of a new common adversary. Periods of peace based on equilibrium often have been no more than prolonged armistices. The struggle for justice within nations or between them justified in and of itself, is not always a pacific action — it eventually leads to violence.

*   *   *

I do not claim to judge the peace research institutes. I have wanted simply to recall that we know little about the causes of war when it comes to making practical use of such knowledge in order to maintain the peace. I have briefly isolated two theories still in vogue concerning first the arms race and second international economic ambitions.

I have neither condemned arms control, because there are many forms of it, nor have I suggested that SALT II should not be ratified. I have not wanted to enter into the debates of today. Any judgment for or against ratification should require a complete study of the text and analysis of the political as well as the military considerations. My purpose has been to make clear the paradoxes of the doctrine of arms control.

Some facts are obvious, irrefutable. We recall the official goals of arms control. Reduce the risk of war: I see no improvement. Reduce the destruction if, in spite of everything, a war should occur: the destruction would perhaps be even worse because the superpowers have eliminated their means of defence and increased the means of offence — the number of warheads and the throw-weight of the heavy missiles. Reduction of military spending: since SALT I, both sides have increased their budgets for strategic weapons, the Soviet Union much more than the United States. Jimmy Carter had promised a massive increase of spending on the MX and the Trident if SALT II were ratified. Ronald Reagan will do it with or without ratification.

Why the spectacular failure? I have exposed some reasons which I will summarize in different language.

Is real agreement regarding the balance of military forces possible between states which remain fundamentally hostile to each other? They could agree against nuclear proliferation, but each one of them is in search of a parity favorable to it.

Beyond this primitive reason, I would mention technical progress. The first yardstick is the number of launchers, but you may put many warheads in any missile. Then comes firing accuracy, which transforms the efficiency and function of the missiles. The missiles become more vulnerable and, at the same time, battlefield weapons (warheads of low yield). 'Equivalence' becomes more and more difficult to establish. One has to take into consideration the pay-load, the throw-weight, the accuracy of the missile, and the yield of the warhead.

The third argument, the most political, the most instructive, is the fallacy of partial stability. Partial stability might compromise global stability, especially because of the asymmetry between the two camps. I even distinguish three styles of asymmetry:

1. Nuclear weapons have not necessarily the same place in the defence systems of the two camps; the Soviet camp maintains its superiority in the domain of conventional weaponry. Equivalence at the highest level may bring about the inferiority of one side in the global balance.

2. The asymmetry of the two nuclear systems makes equivalence at least equivocal. The Soviet camp is superior in throw-weight, in megatonnage; the American in number of warheads. Which is more important? What are the consequences of the Soviet capability of destroying the land-based launchers, the ICBM's? How does the nuclear strategic balance influence the minds of the statesmen and the course of diplomacy?

3. The present accuracy of the missiles gives the camp which strikes first an enormous advantage. The political asymmetry between a fragile coalition of democracies and the unified control

of the Eastern armies determines, in advance, who will strike first. Are the Pershing II and the cruise missiles invulnerable enough to balance the SS-20?

There may be a fourth asymmetry. Do the Soviet military leaders consider the use of nuclear weapons in battle normal, inevitable? For what sorts of hostilities do they prepare their troops? And do the political leaders really adhere to the doctrine revealed in the books of their generals, according to which a nuclear war could be won like any war of the past?

Thirty years ago we tended to believe that the states would modify their behaviour in response to the threat of nuclear arms. Instead, these arms have been integrated into the course of ordinary international relations, with one new element, the fear of escalation to extremes and nuclear wars. The states, the cold monsters, have not changed, they have become more prudent. Scientific studies on war, conducted by institutes of polemics, peace, or strategy, have made no decisive contribution to the task of the statesmen. It is up to the statesmen to know whether the SALT negotiations are politically desirable, however modest their military results. And it is up to them also to know whether SALT is necessary for detente, or whether detente must lead to SALT, or whether detente is necessary to peace.

I have focussed on two questions: are states which are basically hostile to each other able to come to an essential agreement about the relationship between their forces? My reply is no. Have we learnt the causes of war and the means of preventing it? Here again, my reply is no. Since complex societies have existed, this has been the historical condition of mankind. So far technology has turned weaponry upside down, but not men. Should we be surprised? Should we despair? Neither surprised nor despairing. The human adventure, horrible and glorious, goes on.

The Arms Race

JOAN ROBINSON

THE TANNER LECTURES ON HUMAN VALUES

Delivered at
The University of Utah

April 14 and 16, 1981

JOAN ROBINSON was educated at Girton College, University of Cambridge, where she was a Gilchrist scholar. After a period in India she joined the Cambridge faculty in economics in 1931. In 1965 she was elected to a professorial fellowship at Newnham and made an honorary Fellow of Girton; she became an honorary Fellow of Newnham in 1971. Professor Robinson has attempted to form a unified system of political economy directly applicable to the analysis of policy problems in the modern world, and she actively participated in the formation and propagation of the Keynesian revolution. Her diverse bibliography includes *The Economics of Imperfect Competition* (1933), *Introduction to the Theory of Employment* (1937), *The Accumulation of Capital* (1956), *Economic Philosophy* (1962), *Freedom and Necessity* (1970), and *Economic Heresies* (1971). Joan Robinson died in late summer, 1983.

I

Fanciful scientists have discussed the possibility of colonising the solar system, but meanwhile we have only one world and we have created a situation which threatens to make it uninhabitable. When I say *we* I am referring to the generation of the human race now extant, led and manipulated by the ruling powers of the great industrial nations. The peril threatening the world arises from a technological development in warfare. Over the centuries wars have been growing more and more destructive, but up till now it was always possible to restore the economic base of the countries concerned after the war was over. From nuclear destruction there is no recovery.

This has been proved both by a priori calculations and by an actual demonstration. A large area in the Urals in Russia was ruined by an accidental explosion (believed to have been in a deposit of waste nuclear fuel), which not only destroyed all man-made structures and all animal and vegetable life but rendered the place uninhabitable and uncultivatable for hundreds of years, if not forever.

The exploitation of nuclear power threatens not only the basis of the livelihood of mankind but also human life itself.

> In view of the threat that nuclear technology poses to the ecosphere, we must acknowledge that Homo sapiens has reached an evolutionary turning point. Thousands of tons of radioactive materials, released by nuclear explosions and reactor spills, are now dispersing through the environment. Nonbiodegradable, and some potent virtually forever, these toxic materials will continue to accumulate, and eventually their effects on the biosphere and on human beings will be grave: many people will begin to develop and die of cancer; or their reproductive genes will mutate, resulting in an in-

creased incidence of congenitally deformed and diseased off-
spring — not just in the next generation, but for the rest of
time. An all-out nuclear war would kill millions of people and
accelerate these biological hazards among the survivors: the
earth would be poisoned and laid waste, rendered uninhabitable for aeons.[1]

Dr. Helen Caldicott includes the effects of accidents from nuclear
power stations in this warning. The pros and cons of civilian use
of nuclear power is a subject that I cannot go into here, but I must
object that those who glibly protest that coal mining is also dangerous have not taken in the point. The damage caused by nuclear
poison is not just to some unlucky individuals but to the pool of
genes to be passed on to future generations. The peril is not just
to us, who are alive today, but to the human race itself.

The stockpile of arms in the world today provides: "enough
firepower . . . to destroy every city on earth seven times over. Still,
the arms race continues, the weapons multiply and become more
specialized, and the likelihood of their utilization grows. . . . Countries, driven by fear and a mutual distrust bordering on the patho-
logical, are locked into a suicidal strategy calling, in the words of
the Pentagon, for 'mutually assured destruction' (MAD) as the
best deterrent to war. But 'arms for peace' and 'security through
mass genocide' are strategies that defy logic and common sense.
They epitomize our nuclear madness." [2]

How has this situation been allowed to arise? Mainly, I suppose, because the whole subject is so horrifying that we prefer not
to think about it and, in each country, leave the notions of various so-called experts and the interplay of various vested interests
to shape our history for us. But just not to think about it makes
it all the more dangerous.

[1] Helen Caldicott, with the assistance of Nancy Herrington and Nahum Stiskin,
Nuclear Madness: What You Can Do! (New York: Autumn Press, 1979), p. 17.
[2] Ibid., p. 83.

Before we begin, one point must be made clear. Military expenditure in each country goes under the heading of "defense." This is a misnomer. In the case of nuclear missiles there is no defense possible. (Perhaps the development of lasers is going to change the situation, but that is not in sight yet.)

Earl Mountbatten, shortly before he was murdered by an Irish fanatic, issued this warning to the world:

> A military confrontation between the nuclear powers could entail the horrifying risk of nuclear warfare. The Western powers and the USSR started by producing and stockpiling nuclear weapons as a deterrent to general war. The idea seemed simple enough. Because of the enormous amount of destruction that could be wreaked by a single nuclear explosion, the idea was that both sides in what we still see as an East–West conflict would be deterred from taking any aggressive action which might endanger the vital interests of the other.
>
> It was not long, however, before smaller nuclear weapons of various designs were produced and deployed for use in what was assumed to be a tactical or theatre war. The belief was that were hostilities ever to break out in Western Europe, such weapons could be used in field warfare without triggering an all-out nuclear exchange leading to the final holocaust.
>
> I have never found this idea credible. I have never been able to accept the reasons for the belief that any class of nuclear weapons can be categorised in terms of their tactical or strategic purposes. . . .
>
> I know how impossible it is to pursue military operations in accordance with fixed plans and agreements. In warfare the unexpected is the rule and no one can anticipate what an opponent's reaction will be to the unexpected.
>
> . . . .
>
> I repeat in all sincerity as a military man I can see no use for any nuclear weapons which would not end in escalation, with consequences that no one can conceive.
>
> And nuclear devastation is not science fiction — it is a matter of fact. Thirty-four years ago there was the terrifying

experience of the two atomic bombs that effaced the cities of Hiroshima and Nagasaki off the map.

. . . .

We remember the tens and thousands who were killed instantly or worse still those who suffered a slow painful death from the effect of the burns — we forget that many are still dying horribly from the delayed effects of radiation. To this knowledge must be added the fact that we now have missiles a thousand times as dreadful; I repeat, a thousand times as horrible.

. . . .

A new world war can hardly fail to involve the all-out use of nuclear weapons. Such a war would not drag on for years. It could all be over in a matter of a day.

And when it is all over what will the world be like? Our fine great buildings, our homes will exist no more. The thousands of years it took to develop our civilisation will have been in vain. Our works of art will be lost. Radio, television, newspapers will disappear. There will be no hospitals. No help can be expected for the few mutilated survivors in any town to be sent from a neighbouring town — there will be no neighbouring towns left, no neighbours, there will be no help, there will be no hope.

. . . .

As a military man who has given half a century of active Service I say in all sincerity that the nuclear arms race has no military purpose. Wars cannot be fought with nuclear weapons. Their existence only adds to our perils because of the illusions which they have generated.

There are powerful voices around the world who still give credence to the old Roman precept — if you desire peace, prepare for war. This is absolute nuclear nonsense and I repeat — it is a disastrous misconception to believe that by increasing the total uncertainty one increases one's own certainty.

. . . .

After all it is true that science offers us almost unlimited opportunities, but it is up to us, the people, to make the moral and philosophical choices and since the threat to humanity is the work of human beings, it is up to man to save himself from himself.

The world now stands on the brink of the final Abyss. Let us all resolve to take all possible practical steps to ensure that we do not, through our own folly, go over the edge.

Earl Mountbatten was a cousin of the Queen of England. He was one of the few survivors of the First World War who rose to high command (in the British navy) in the Second. As Chief of the British Defense Staff he was in charge of the preparations for the invasion of Europe in 1944. He could not be dismissed as a deluded left-wing intellectual or a starry-eyed pacifist, but he did not have much influence on British policy.

When the question of siting neutron bombs in Europe came up in February of 1980, the British Prime Minister "made an indirect appeal to the Netherlands to allow new nuclear missiles to be based on Dutch soil. 'If you value your way of life — the freedoms we have in the West — you must be prepared to defend it. New nuclear weapons are necessary because of the concentration of them in the Soviet Union," Mrs. Thatcher said.[3]

The nuclear weapons that are now being developed cannot provide defense. If they are not to be used for aggression they could only be used for revenge. This was forcibly illustrated for us in Cambridgeshire when there was a false alarm last summer. In eastern England automatic gadgets are set up which are intended to give a warning signal when a rocket is detected on its way. This was set off by (I think) a flight of geese. Immediately, from the surrounding aerodromes, loaded planes shot into the air, ready to fly east and drop bombs over there. Their function was evidently not defense but retaliation. What satisfaction would it be, when our homeland was destroyed, to go and destroy the homeland of a supposed enemy? It is certainly a misnomer to describe this as defense.

[3] *Guardian* (London), February 7, 1980.

The horror, the lack of logic, and the isolation due to rules of secrecy produce strange aberrations of thought: a high-ranking officer in the Air Defence Command is reported as saying in 1952 that "it was not really our policy" to attempt to defend American civilians against atomic attack "for that is so big a job that it would interfere with our retaliatory capabilities." [4]

Far from contributing to defense, the production of weapons increases peril. A quaint system has developed of announcing that some new horror will be available in three or five years' time, so that if the other side is as hostile and aggressive as our propaganda pretends, they would be well advised to "take it out," as the phrase is, before it can be installed.

Perhaps in the deepest sense we can never understand our own history, but it seems to me to be worthwhile to try to discuss how this dangerous situation has arisen. I suggest three aspects — the Cold War, the momentum of research and development, and the connection of armaments with the problem of employment. I will take up the last topic in my second lecture. The first two will be opened up today.

First, the Cold War. The kaleidoscope of history has brought into existence two great national powers, each with its troop of allies and satellites. This would in any case have been a cause of tension and rivalry, but it so happens that they support two different ideologies — so-called communism in the Eastern camp and so-called freedom in the West — which gives the conflict between them something of the character of the wars of religion. This makes conflict intractable. On both sides, propaganda and indoctrination are used to cover sectional interests, but at bottom there is a solid core of genuine conviction. In the West, we are taught that *our* side stands for noble ideals and *theirs* for evil. *We* must keep up the struggle to save the world from *them*. Any

[4] Peter Goodchild, *J. Robert Oppenheimer* (London: B.B.C., 1980), p. 219; published in America as *Robert Oppenheimer: Shatterer of Worlds* (New York: Houghton Mifflin, 1981).

suggestion of relaxation or compromise, unless it can be shown to tell in *our* favour, is seen as treachery.

The conflict of ideologies smothers self-criticism. The wisest thing that ever was said about politics is, "Look for the beam in your own eye before a mote in the eye of your opponent." Where a clash of faiths is involved the instinctive response is, "But it is they, not we, who have a beam in the eye." This is most damaging to the side that professes freedom as its ideology, for obscurantism and self-righteousness are liable to tarnish that very openness and objectivity which is supposed to be the glory of the Western side.

The self-righteousness and mutual distrust induced by the atmosphere of a war of ideology has been an element in preventing agreement between the two halves of the divided world to eliminate atomic weapons. The very process of building up destructive power contributed to keeping ideological conflict alive. It is clear that for a nation that has an enemy, it is necessary to arm, but it is also true that if a nation has arms it is necessary to have an enemy. To justify armaments, fear and tension have been kept up and each side makes use of the other as a bogy.

The second, and perhaps the main cause of the situation we have got ourselves into is the momentum of research and development. When an idea has once been started it must be pursued without regard to consequences, and once a new weapon or means of attack has been perfected it is extremely difficult to prevent it being added to the stock of means of destruction. The clearest case of this that we have seen so far in the atomic sphere is one of the earliest — the bombing of Nagasaki.

The report that Hitler was developing an atomic bomb activated the Allies to reply in kind. General Groves was the military director of the project and Robert Oppenheimer was in charge of the scientific work. In 1944 it became clear that the German project had been abandoned. One of the American scientists at Los Alamos made the comment to another "If the Germans don't have the bomb then we won't need to use ours." "You don't know

Groves" was the reply. "If we have such a weapon, then we will use it." [5]

In May 1945 Germany surrendered before the work on the bomb had been completed but there was still Japan. On 16th July 1945 a bomb was tested in the desert at Alamogordo. The story from that date till the surrender of Japan is the subject of a dispute that has recently been revived.[6] The Japanese army had not been decisively defeated in the wide ranging war in Asia and was now concentrated in Japan. The Allies had decided that an invasion of Japan would be necessary to finish the war. One side in the dispute is based on the argument that the Japanese would have made a desperate suicidal defense which would have cost 500,000 to 750,000 American casualties. On this view, the surrender of Japan was due to the bomb on Hiroshima, which can thus be credited with saving American lives. Joseph Alsop, who supports this side of the argument, maintains that it saved Japanese lives as well because the casualties, military and civilian, caused by an invasion accompanied by "normal" bombing would have been greater than those caused by the atomic bombs.

In the other version of the story, supported by David Joravsky, the suicidal fanaticism of Japanese officers was due to personal loyalty to the Emperor which was threatened by the demand for unconditional surrender. There was a peace party in Japan, supported by the Emperor himself. An official mission had been sent to Moscow in the spring of 1945 to ask Stalin to negotiate terms of surrender. Stalin refused to help. He wanted to keep Japan in the war long enough to permit the invasion of Manchuria, which was set for August tenth, just as the Western allies needed to postpone the surrender until the bomb was ready to be used. On this version the Japanese peace party would have prevailed, at any time after the spring of 1945, provided they had been told that

[5] Ibid., p. 111.
[6] *New York Review of Books*, October 23, 1980, and February 18, 1981.

"unconditional surrender" did not rule out retaining the Emperor. On this version, Hiroshima had nothing to do with it.

My friend and colleague Professor Tsuru, at that time a junior member of the Japanese foreign office, was on the unsuccessful mission to Moscow. He does not support Joravsky. His judgement[7] is that resistance by the Japanese army would have been desperate and would have taken at least a month to overcome, with heavy casualties.

But the story was much more complicated than Alsop allows. The momentum of research was kept up by competition and rivalry *within* home arms production on both sides. Herbert York in the *Advisors* tells the story of the struggle between Teller and Oppenheimer over the hydrogen bomb, which Teller unfortunately won.

There were two different kinds of fission weapons being developed at Los Alamos. One using U235 and the other plutonium. "The design of the U235 bomb was based on particularly simple and straight-forward principles. The plutonium bomb was based on more novel design principles." It was the plutonium bomb which was tested, successfully, at Alamogordo on July sixteenth. On August sixth Hiroshima was wiped out with the U235 bomb. Hiroshima has given its name to the horror of the epoch that we are now living in and it can be credited with precipitating the surrender of Japan. The plutonium bomb had been tested and was known to work. Why then was it dropped on Nagasaki? What was the point of this overkill?

At the time, several of the European scientists who had contributed to producing the bomb were quite unhappy. Niels Bohr in particular campaigned against its being used unannounced, but he was brushed aside. Otto Frisch, who came to England as a refugee from Hitler, discusses his own attitude.

> Some of us said that scientists ought to put their weight behind what they felt to be the right course of action; others

[7] In a personal letter.

took the line that the cobbler should stick to his last. I remember a story being told about the Greek sculptor Phidias who had completed a new statue of Zeus and hidden behind it to hear what the passing Athenians said. When he heard a cobbler say "The big toe is too large" he came back later at night and chipped a bit off the big toe. The next morning he saw the cobbler pass again, remarking that the toe had been improved but the elbow wasn't right. At that, Phidias stepped out from his hiding place and addressed the cobbler with the words, "When you talk about toes you talk about what you know, and I listen; but I pay no attention when you talk about elbows." The moral being, of course, that scientists should stick to matters of their own competence, and at the time I found that view very plausible. I am no longer convinced that this is always right. Scientists are trained to think objectively and dispassionately, an asset for making decisions of any kind.

We didn't know when the bomb would be dropped in earnest or where it would be dropped. Then one day, some three weeks after Alamogordo, there was a sudden noise in the laboratory, of running footsteps and yelling voices. Somebody opened my door and shouted "Hiroshima has been destroyed!"; about a hundred thousand people were thought to have been killed. I still remember the feeling of unease, indeed nausea, when I saw how many of my friends were rushing to the telephone to book tables at the La Fonda hotel in Santa Fe, in order to celebrate. Of course they were exalted by the success of their work, but it seemed rather ghoulish to celebrate the sudden death of a hundred thousand people, even if they were 'enemies'. On the other hand there was the argument that this slaughter had saved the lives of many more Americans *and* Japanese who would have died in the slow process of conquest by which the war might have had to be ended had there been no atom bomb. But few of us could see any moral reason for dropping a second bomb (on Nagasaki) only a few days later, even though that brought the war to an immediate halt. Most of us thought that the Japanese would have surrendered within a few days anyhow. But this is a subject that has been endlessly debated and never settled.[8]

[8] Otto Frisch, *What Little I Remember* (Cambridge: Cambridge University Press, 1979), pp. 176–77.

It has not been settled yet. A clue lies in the date.[9] August tenth, the day after Nagasaki, had been agreed on as the date for the Soviet invasion of Manchuria. The invasion was completely successful but all the limelight fell on the bomb. Here the two aspects of our situation, the wars of religion and the momentum of research, combine. In popular opinion, Japan was conquered by American technology, not by Russian military might.

From then on even the pretence of alliance and cooperation between the great powers was abandoned.

The era of the cold war had begun.

Robert Oppenheimer agonised over his responsibility for Hiroshima. In 1951 his rival, Edward Teller, was working on the next generation of means of devastation, the hydrogen bomb. Oppenheimer opposed it and, presumably for that reason, a case was fabricated for questioning his loyalty. He gave way, however, to the momentum of research. The new conception was "technically so sweet you could not argue about that." "You go ahead and do it and you argue about what to do about it only after you have had your technical success." [10] Here is the clearest statement of the process which has brought us to where we are.

In 1945, unbeknownst to the West, the Russians were working upon a bomb of their own, a goal they achieved in 1949. (How much help they got from information passed to them by so-called traitors among the Western scientists is not known, but presumably they would have in any case caught up very soon.)

Lord Zuckermann, in his masterly analysis of the role of scientific advisors to governments,[11] laments their failure to inhibit the arms race. "It need not have happened but it did." Zuckermann argues that the race started in 1946 with the refusal of the USSR

[9] See P. M. S. Blackett, *Fear, War and the Bomb* (New York: McGraw-Hill, 1947).

[10] Goodchild, op. cit., p. 210.

[11] "Science Advisors and Scientific Advisors," *Proceedings of the American Philosophical Society*, vol. 24, no. 4 (August 1979), reproduced as a pamphlet (London: Menard Press, 1980).

to agree to the Lilienthal plan for placing all nuclear technology —
military and civil — under UN control.

Behind this refusal lay the force of the war of ideologies. The
influence of the West in the United Nations was much greater
than that of the Russians and they refused to accept a position
of military and industrial inferiority, protected only by a treaty.

In the West, according to Zuckermann,

> Fears of Russian capabilities and intentions became acute when
> the first Sputnik was launched in 1957, and, correspondingly,
> the Russians became increasingly fearful of the intentions of
> the West. Warnings that the Russians were well ahead of the
> U.S.A. in the size of their nuclear missile armoury — warnings
> of a so-called 'missile gap', which we now know did not exist—
> started to be fostered, and became a powerful political card in
> the run-up to the 1960 Presidential election. A race into space
> was launched. Throughout this period both sides were testing
> nuclear warheads in the atmosphere, with the U.K. participat-
> ing on its own, but to a lesser extent. Very soon there was
> world-wide concern about the serious health hazards associated
> with radioactive fall-out. Formal diplomatic and technical
> talks were started in Geneva to consider an international agree-
> ment to ban all tests.[12]

Zuckermann, who was involved in the discussions, tells us that
President Eisenhower and then Kennedy wanted a ban on all
tests, and there were some signs that gave reason to believe that
Khrushchev had the same goal in mind.

> Unfortunately there was also acute opposition to any treaty.
> Regardless of the world-wide and, from the scientific point of
> view, thoroughly justified concern about fall-out, there were in
> fact many — including prominent scientists in the weapons
> laboratories — who were opposed to any ban on atmospheric
> tests, leave alone an end to the elaboration of new warheads.
> Their "hawkish" views carried considerable weight among the
> military, in congressional committees, and in some sections of

---

[12] Ibid.

the public, who soon became persuaded that there was something to be gained by continuing the nuclear arms race, and that anyhow the Russians would be bound to cheat, whatever treaty was agreed.[13]

It soon became clear that the Senate would not ratify a treaty for a total test ban unless humiliating terms (on-site inspection) were imposed upon the Russians, which they would obviously not accept.

Herbert York, an insider who, before he resigned, was Director of Defense Research in the Pentagon, wrote, in his powerful book *Race to Oblivion*, that one of the political prices that the President had to pay for even a partial test ban in 1963 "was a promise that the Atomic Energy Commission would embark on a programme of underground tests vigorous enough 'to satisfy all our military requirements'." [14]

Zuckermann maintains that the top scientific advisors understood the situation very well but they have been continuously frustrated by the momentum of research. A system has developed in which the military chiefs merely serve as a channel through which the men in the laboratories transmit their views.

The pressure from the laboratories has been assisted by exaggerated accounts of the Soviet threat. York refers to a steady flow of "phony intelligence" from a variety of sources, and tells us that "those who had all the facts of the matter and knew there was no real basis for any of these claims [i.e., about Russian intentions and capacities] were hamstrung in any attempts being made to deal with them by the secrecy which always surrounds real intelligence information."

Why then has all the authoritative testimony on these matters from respected and highly informed scientists been set aside over the past two decades? Why, instead, have the nuclear bomb enthusiasts been heeded? "The guilty men and organizations,"

13 Ibid.
14 Herbert York, *Race to Oblivion*.

writes York, "are to be found at all levels of government and in all segments of society: Presidents, Presidential candidates; governors and mayors, members of Congress, civilian officials and military officers; business executives and labour leaders, famous scientists and run-of-the-mill engineers; writers and editorialists; and just plain folks." Their motives, he tells us, are various, but "nearly all such individuals," he goes on to say,

> have had a deep long-term involvement in the arms race. They derive either their incomes, their profits, or their consultant fees from it. But much more important than money as a motivating force are the individuals' own psychic and spiritual needs; the majority of the key individual promoters of the arms race derive a very large part of their self-esteem from their participation in what they believe to be an essential — even holy — cause. . . . They are inspired by ingenious and clever ideas, challenged by bold statements of real and imaginary military requirements, stimulated to match or exceed technological progress by the other side or even by a rival military service here at home, and victimized by rumours and phony intelligence. Some have been lured by the siren call of rapid advancement, personal recognition, and unlimited opportunity, and some have been bought by promises of capital gains. Some have sought out and even made up problems to fit the solution they have spent much of their lives discovering and developing. A few have used the arms race to achieve other, often hidden objectives.[15]

On the Soviet side, perhaps, some elements in the psychological situation may be different, but apparently the consequences are much the same.

Zuckermann's argument is unanswerable but it has not had much success.

"It seems all but incredible that the battle which the presidential science advisors have waged with those who participated technically in the race at operational levels below their own seems

[15] Ibid., p. 235.

to have been a lost cause from the start. All the presidential science advisors and the Directors of Defense Research and Engineering with whom I have discussed the problem," he writes,

> recognise that once the threshold of mutual nuclear deterrence has been crossed, there is no technical sense in the further elaboration or multiplication of nuclear weapon systems. But this is not the point of view that has got across. Instead, their opponents knew how to respond to the mood of the country, how to capture the attention of the media, how to stir the hearts of generals. They have been adept at taking the short-term view and in creating the climate within which political chiefs have to operate. The longer term view of the top advisors — that the arms race feeds itself, that there is no technical solution to the problem of defence against nuclear weapons — that view is too difficult to put across, strangely, I believe, not because it sounds soft and defeatist, but because it is too simple and too logical, and because the basic facts have become submerged in a sea of acronyms and numbers, a sea of MIRVs, of particle beams, of "throw-weights," and so on. And the political chiefs whom the chief science advisors serve, and who are only in office for brief periods, inevitably find themselves in situations that leave little room for manoeuvre — situations characterised by an inertia and a resistance to change which is only to be expected when hundreds of thousands of the electors on whom they depend are making their livings doing things which were promoted years before by their political predecessors. It is the past which imbues the arms race with its inner momentum.[16]

Under the partial test ban underground experiments went on and the stockpile of means of destruction in the world continued to grow, but alarm was reduced by the theory of a "balance of terror." It was obvious that neither side could conceivably survive the exchange that would follow a "first strike" and so both were "deterred" from striking.

---

[16] Zuckermann, op. cit.

During the 1970's research and development continued. Technological advance went into improving the accuracy of aim of rockets and the secrecy with which a sudden attack could be launched. These new devices are designed for aggression. The notion of defense has faded from the scene. In particular, the neutron bomb, which is designed to wipe out the defenders of a city with a minimum of damage to buildings, seems to be designed for the requirements of a conqueror.

Now, instead of deterrence we have competition in terror. Each invention introduced on one side has to be copied on the other. In public discussion this reaches the height of absurdity when there is a rumour that the other side is disregarding an agreement not to produce poison gas. If *they* are going to do so, *we* must do so. In 1938 and 1939, every man, woman, and child in the United Kingdom was issued a gasmask. This would be a more intelligent response to the threat if it turned out to be actual. It seems that the technicians regard agreements that limit their activities as a nuisance and eagerly seize upon any excuse to abrogate them.

The title of the last chapter in York's book is "The Ultimate Absurdity":

> The actions and processes described in this book have led to two absurd situations.
>
> The first of these absurdities has been with us for some time, and has come to be widely recognized for what it is. It lies in the fact that ever since World War II the military power of the United States has been steadily increasing, while at the same time our national security has been rapidly and inexorably decreasing. The same thing is happening to the Soviet Union.
>
> The second of these absurdities is still in an early stage and, for reasons of secrecy, is not yet so widely recognized as the first. It lies in the fact that in the United States the power to decide whether or not doomsday has arrived is in the process of passing from statesmen and politicians to lower-level officers and technicians and, eventually, to machines.

Machines such as the warning system which I mentioned that was set off by a flight of geese.

Official pronouncements made in the West and discussed in the media seem to be mainly aimed at providing soothing syrup to discourage the general public from forming any opinion in this situation; when some warnings are emitted, they are mainly confined (apart from Mountbatten's) to the loss of life that could be caused by nuclear war. This seems to be a kind of collective egoism. What is at risk is not just the lives of the present generation of the inhabitants of the northern hemisphere or of the whole globe, it is, as Mountbatten recognised, the continuance of our civilization. No doubt that civilization, East and West together, is imperfect, bloodstained, full of injustice, but all the same it is a great achievement and full of new possibilities. We surely should be concerned not to throw it away? Supposing that we squeak through the present era of crisis and manage to survive for twenty or fifty years, we should still leave the world in peril of a future disaster. Unless mankind can give up the habit of making national wars, it seems that sooner or later it will destroy itself.

> After such knowledge, what forgiveness? Think now
> History has many cunning passages, contrived corridors
> And issues, deceives with whispering ambitions,
> Guides us by vanities. Think now
> She gives when our attention is distracted
> And what she gives, gives with such supple confusions
> That the giving famishes the craving. Gives too late
> What's not believed in, or if still believed,
> In memory only, reconsidered passion. Gives too soon
> Into weak hands, what's thought can be dispensed with
> Till the refusal propagates a fear. Think
> Neither fear nor courage saves us. Unnatural vices
> Are fathered by our heroism. Virtues
> Are forced upon us by our impudent crimes.
> These tears are shaken from the wrath-bearing tree.
>
> T. S. Eliot, *Gerontion*

II

In my first lecture I tried to open up the discussion of two aspects of the perpetuation of the arms race: the element of a war of religion in the conflict between so-called communism in the East and so-called freedom in the West and the momentum of research and development which seems to be making it impossible to halt and reverse the process even when it has become obvious that there can be no end to the dispute except mutual destruction. The third aspect to be discussed is the connection between the arms race and the principle of effective demand.

The Keynesian revolution in economic theory which emerged from the great slump of the 1930's is often identified merely with a policy of running a budget deficit to reduce unemployment; but it was more than that. It was a great gain in insight into the manner of operation of a capitalist industrial economy. The *principle of effective demand* means that the accumulation of capital in the sense of productive capacity is not directly due to saving in terms of money — finance — but to investment in creating physical means of production. It can be discussed in terms of the old distinction, drawn by Alfred Marshall, between short- and long-period effects.

At any moment, in each country, there is in existence a certain stock of means of production and transport — factories, railways, shipping, and so forth; housing and commercial and educational establishments, a certain distribution of finance, and a labour force of certain skills and capacities. These are the long-period factors. The level of utilisation of this productive capacity depends on short-period influences, in particular on the overall level of expenditure. In a modern industrial economy, there is almost no production for self-consumption except housework within the home, and even that is growing less and less. Everyone's income, therefore, depends on other people's expenditures. If there was no expenditure this month except out of last month's income, the system would quickly run down. Not all income is spent. Some is

used to pay off debts and some is saved to add to private wealth or
financial reserves of businesses. On the other hand, some expenditure this month is covered from wealth earned and saved earlier
and some is financed by borrowing — by businesses, households,
and government institutions. The aim of business investment is to
provide an enlarged capacity for earning more profit in the future.
When it is successful it becomes an addition to the capital of the
business. But even investment which does not turn out to be
profitable supports employment while it is going on.

In the slump of the thirties, the advocates of public loan
expenditure were mocked by the argument that they were advocat-
ing the policy of paying workers to dig holes in the ground and
fill them up again. They replied that wages are spent on goods
and services. The excess of what a family can buy when the bread-
winner is earning over what they spend when he is on the dole
calls into being a genuine increase in real national income.

But Keynes himself gave a confusing account of the point.
He sometimes seemed to argue that unproductive investment is
actually to be preferred to useful investment.

> If — for whatever reason — the rate of interest cannot
> fall as fast as the marginal efficiency of capital would fall with
> a rate of accumulation corresponding to what the community
> would choose to save at a rate of interest equal to the marginal
> efficiency of capital in conditions of full employment, then
> even a diversion of the desire to hold wealth towards assets,
> which will in fact yield no economic fruits whatever, will
> increase economic well-being. In so far as millionaires find
> their satisfaction in building mighty mansions to contain their
> bodies when alive and pyramids to shelter them after death, or,
> repenting of their sins, erect cathedrals and endow monasteries
> or foreign missions, the day when abundance of capital will
> interfere with abundance of output may be postponed. "To
> dig holes in the ground," paid for out of savings, will increase,
> not only employment, but the real national dividend of useful
> goods and services. It is not reasonable, however, that a
> sensible community should be content to remain dependent

on such fortuitous and often wasteful mitigations when once
we understand the influences upon which effective demand
depends.[1]

This suggests that there is only a certain amount of productive
equipment that is worth having and that accumulation beyond
this point is actually worse than useless. This argument was part
of the old theory from which Keynes had "a long struggle to
escape" — the concept of a static "schedule of marginal efficiency
of capital." In real life investment creates new outlets for itself
by technical inventions and the introduction of new commodities.
(The great slump of the thirties was partly relieved by the massive
demand generated by the revolution in means of transport set
going by the motor car.)

Moreover, even in the wealthiest country, there are families
who feel themselves to be living at too low a standard of life who
would be happy to spend more money on goods and services if
only they had it.

Keynes was thinking narrowly in terms of the problems of the
industrialised West. Nowadays we are becoming conscious of the
enormous needs of the impoverished Third World. In Africa in
particular the growth of numbers ahead of agricultural development is posing a huge problem which from time to time comes to
the surface in outright famine here or there in that continent.
There is no lack of need for investment or of know-how for
designing it. The impediments that stand in the way are political
and financial, not technical or economic.

It is not a limitation of useful ideas or schemes for investment
projects but the religious belief in laisser-faire in the Western
world that stands in the way of systematic employment policy.

In the 1930's, unbeknownst to Keynes, the principle of effective demand had been discovered independently in defeated Ger-

[1] John Maynard Keynes, *The General Theory of Employment, Interest and Money*
(1936), pp. 219–20.

many; not only discovered but actually put into practice. Nicholas Kaldor was recently celebrating the eightieth birthday of an unknown prophet, H.-J. Rüstow, whom he places with Maynard Keynes and Michael Kalecki as one of the independent discoverers of what we now know as the theory of employment.

The German economy, still groggy after the great inflation of 1923, was hit by the full force of the Great Depression in 1931. In the words of H.-J. Rüstow,

> At that time there were a number of businessmen, economists with practical experience and some non-academic theoretical economists who maintained that such large-scale unemployment could only be overcome by large-scale public works; members of this group repeatedly put forward concrete plans for stimulating the economy by such means. The academic establishment, on the other hand, asserted, almost without exception, that the inherent equilibrating forces of the market economy would cure the disease, whilst any interference with this "natural recuperative process" would serve to make the situation worse, and the adoption of any of the proposed programmes for putting the unemployment to work would cause renewed inflation.
>
>   . . .
>
> Gradually, investment dropped to only one-third of its previous level and was no longer sufficient even to maintain existing productive capacity intact, let alone generate any accumulation of capital out of profits. This situation led to a cumulative shut-down of less efficient plants and to mass redundancy of labour . . . so that by 1932 no less than 40% of previously employed workers were unemployed. In fact, the true number of unemployed was estimated to be at least one million larger than the six million registered at the labour exchanges. I disagreed with the generally accepted view of the academic profession that the crisis could, or would, be overcome with the normal instruments of a market economy. For even with a very low rate of interest — the level of interest was still at 7% at the beginning of 1932 — entrepreneurs would not have had the incentive to invest on the scale necessary to bring about a

substantial reduction in unemployment. Nor could the problem
be effectively tackled by government work-creation schemes,
even if drawn up on a grand and generous scale. For that
purpose, the schemes would have had to take on a dimension
that would have taken them far beyond the range of projects
normally regarded as falling within the scope of public works.[2]

Rüstow worked out a scheme for subsidising investment through
tax credits and at the same time instituted work-creating schemes
which were expanded after Hitler came to power.

> Despite the fact that, in many cases, existing production
> was larger than what could be sold at prices which covered
> costs, the low net cost of employing additional labour was an
> attractive incentive. Those entrepreneurs who did not use the
> scheme faced the prospect of being undercut in competition by
> those who did. Moreover, the production undertaken by newly
> employed labour would mostly be in the nature of stock-
> building. It would take many weeks, or even months, before
> the new output yielded finished consumer goods; the addition
> to employment, meanwhile, brought about an immediate in-
> crease in purchasing power. Thus there would be an improve-
> ment in the cost/receipts relationship in the consumer goods
> sector, which would lead to the re-activation of unused capac-
> ity, raise profits and stimulate increased investment, leading to
> a further improvement in the cost/receipts ratio and thus in
> the level of employment. [p. 415]

Brüning as Chancellor was too much concerned with reparations
to be willing to give it a trial, but when von Papen became Chancellor the scheme was put into operation.

> The course which developments subsequently took was
> fully "according to plan." At the beginning of September, the
> emergency decree implementing the plan came into force, and

[2] H.-J. Rüstow, "The economic crisis of the Weimar Republic and how it was
overcome — a comparison with the present recession," *Cambridge Journal of Economics*, vol. 2, no. 4 (December 1978), p. 414.

during September and October employment increased by 270,000, whereas during the same two months in 1931 it had fallen by 650,000. Entrepreneurs were full of hope, and share prices on the stock exchange shot up. Relative to the production of consumer goods, investment-goods output increased threefold during the first 12 months and sixfold in the first 24 months. Thus the investment/output ratio increased considerably, and the cost/receipts relationship also improved, giving entrepreneurs the profit necessary to sustain a higher level of employment. The re-absorption of the unemployed was so rapid that by October 1934 three million unemployed were back in work. [p. 416]

The plan was still in force when Hitler seized power and it was Hitler who took all the credit for overcoming unemployment.

The gradual increase in the scope of public works programmes undoubtedly had a beneficial effect in accelerating the pace of economic recovery. But the legend that Hitler's construction of motorways (undertaken for military purposes) and the thousands of millions spent on a speedy rearmament programme were the factors which succeeded in abolishing unemployment is unfounded and false in every respect. When Hitler seized power, the economic recovery was already so well advanced that his huge outlays for military purposes were inflationary and could in no way be said to have initiated the disappearance of unemployment. [p. 416]

Rüstow comments, "It is tragic that Brüning did not succeed in eliminating unemployment; had he done so it is almost certain he would not have been overthrown, and not only Germany but the whole world, would have been spared the indescribable misery which National Socialism brought us. But in the last resort, it is not the politicians, but the economic theorists who are to be blamed for the adoption of the wrong policies" (p. 417).

After 1945, it almost seemed for a time as though the lesson had been learned. There was a long run, in the West, of high accumulation, at first set going by Marshall Aid and then taking off on its own. But what about inflation — the continuous rise in the price level in terms of the national currency that nowadays afflicts both rich and poor countries, to a greater or lesser degree? And what about stagflation — the combination of underemployment with rising prices which seems to afflict all the Western industrial nations in lesser or greater degree?

It is important to keep in mind the distinction between the short-run and long-run aspects of the analysis. The short-run aspect concerns the level of employment in a given situation and the degree of utilisation of existing productive capacity while the long-run aspect concerns the change that is going on in the stock of productive capacity and the technique which determines the level of output per man employed.

Understanding has advanced since the *General Theory* was written, though some new confusions have also been introduced. One confusion, which nowadays fortunately seems to be losing its grip in public discussion is *monetarism*, the notion that rising prices and incomes are directly caused by increases in the stock of money — notes, coins, and bank accounts on which checks can be drawn. It requires years of education in economics to grasp this idea, for any sensible person can see that it is merely mistaking a symptom for a cause — when demand is slack, unemployment prevalent, and over-all earnings relatively low, there is less money in circulation at a given level of prices. It is the lack of expenditure which keeps down the quantity of money in circulation, not a limited stock of money that keeps down expenditure.

Another superstition has come up recently — supply-side economics — which seems to suggest that cutting public expenditure will leave more room for private profit-seeking investment, but this is even harder to believe in than monetarism.

Elementary economic teaching is still haunted by the primitive theory of supply and demand. A rise in demand tends to raise prices and increased supply to lower them. It is found nowadays that this is a very misleading account of how industrial prices behave. Richard Kahn summarised the modern analysis:

> Flexible prices are found in those markets for a limited range of primary products where products are homogeneous, demand to the individual producer is almost perfectly elastic, and costs rise with output due to fixed natural resources.
>
> . . .
>
> Fixed or 'sticky' prices are found in manufacturing and distribution, where products are not homogeneous and labour costs are constant or decreasing up to the limits of capacity. The result, which has been well confirmed by various empirical studies and is widely known as Okun's Law, is that productivity in industry increases with short-run increases in output, while prices are sticky.[3]

Prices of manufactures, broadly speaking, are formed by adding a gross margin to the direct costs of wages, materials, and power to cover overhead costs and yield a net profit. When sales are running at levels within the range of expectations, prices are sticky. When demand is such that output runs up to capacity, gross profits are abnormally high but there is not necessarily a rise in prices. It may be more prudent for the manufacturer to enjoy the benefit of good business without grabbing any extra advantage by raising margins. But when demand falls to the point where the pre-fixed margin fails to cover average cost, it becomes necessary to raise it. Thus it is often a fall in sales, rather than a rise, that causes prices to be raised.

This applies to the element in prices that accounts for short-run profits, but the major influences on prices in the short run are wages and material costs. A rise in wage rates leads directly to a rise in prices; when the cost of living, that is, the prices of goods that workers' families consume, is rising, raising wage rates is necessary, for a business cannot keep its labour force working if

---

[3] In "Malinvaud on Keynes," *Cambridge Journal of Economics*, vol. 1, no. 4 (December 1977).

real wages (the purchasing power of money wages over consumer goods) are cut below a certain limit. Thus rising costs raise prices and rising prices raise costs. At the same time, so long as a capitalist economy is prosperous, capital accumulation and technical progress are raising real output per man-week of work. This partly or wholly counter-balances the rise in the money-wage bill. In the prosperous years in the West, inflation was very moderate while real-incomes were rising. It was with the growth of unemployment in the seventies that inflation, set off by the oil crisis in 1973, became a serious nuisance.

There used to be a famous theory — or rather a historical generalisation, known as the Kondratiev cycle — that in the capitalist world there had been a strong tendency, since the late eighteenth century, for the alternation of fourteen to twenty years of high employment and relatively rapid growth and twenty years of slow growth and stagnation.

In the 1970's this theory was revived, but there is no need to be fatalistic. If the economy is going to need a Keynesian boost we should be thinking, rather, to what use our resources should be put. Such views, of course, are abhorrent in the West and seem to throw doubt upon the cult of laisser faire and so-called "freedom" which is the credo of that side in the wars of religion. The preferred method of combating inflation is to cut public expenditure.

The Keynesian thesis is now (in 1981) being illustrated the reverse way round in the U.K. Cutting central and local government expenditure and keeping the sterling exchange rate high so as to encourage imports is increasing unemployment and inhibiting growth.

In so far as increasing unemployment weakens the position of labour in wage bargaining so that rising money-wage rates lag further behind rising prices than when the level of unemployment is higher, this means that some check to rising money prices is won by a sacrifice of real output and growing inequality and bitterness in industrial relations.

I hope you are going to make a very thorough study of the consequences of Mrs. Thatcher's policies in the U.K. before you allow President Reagan to pursue them here.

On the opposite tack, we may ask, is the employment motive playing a part on the Western side in maintaining the arms race? Are we back at the policy of digging holes in the ground to maintain jobs?

Of course the danger of confrontation between the armed giants and the international tensions that it breeds are far and away more important than the problem of unemployment, however grave that may be, but perhaps the problem of employment is playing a minor part in keeping tension alive? To call off the arms race does not require any prior agreement between the two sides. It is open to either great power to state that enough is enough. The initiator has sufficient power to destroy the other side several times over and does not propose to add any more to its stockpile of redundant weapons.

Such an outbreak of common sense in international relations is not to be expected in this mad world, but just for the sake of argument we might enquire whether such a move would have a tendency to precipitate a slump. Some care would have to be taken to prevent a sudden drop in profits and jump in unemployment. Where contracts were broken or legitimate expectations disappointed, the firms concerned should be offered credits on favourable terms and encouraged to switch r and d to constructive forms, in particular the search for new sources of energy. After perhaps a short period of confusion, the effect on employment should be highly favourable. Present policy which combines cutting public expenditure with increasing military investment has introduced a serious distortion into development. From a short-period point of view, man-power, including the most expensively trained scientific man-power, is shifting from services such as health and education and the production of civilian goods in general into production of war-like stores.

Research conducted by one of the big trade unions involved appears to show that when a certain flow of finance is deflected from civilian to military production there is a reduction of employment. The cost of materials handled and allowance for profits is higher per man employed on the average than in civilian branches of industry, so that cost per unit of employment is greater.[4] Moreover, part of the cost is for mining the earth's crust for rare minerals and embodying them in forms that can be used only for destruction.

A switch-back of resources to civilian uses should have correspondingly favourable effects from a short-period point of view.

From a long-period point of view the loss due to the arms race is literally incalculable, for we cannot know what benefits would have been derived from applying the mental and material resources involved to constructive ends.

What form would increased civilian employment take? Emma Rothschild has made a very interesting analysis of the tendency of the structure of employment in the USA to shift from manufacture towards services:

> The 1970s were a time of startlingly rapid expansion in employment in the American economy. In the period of the economic crisis alone, from 1973 to 1979, almost 13 million new nonagricultural jobs were created of which almost 11 million were in the private economy.
>
> The new American jobs were concentrated, however, in two sectors of the private economy—services and retail trade—and, at least in the early 1970s, in one public sector, state and local government. By 1979, 43 percent of all Americans employed in the private nonagricultural economy worked in services and retail trade. The two sectors together provided more than 70 percent of all new private jobs created from 1973 to the summer of 1980.
>
> Even within these two vast sectors, the growth in employment was further concentrated. Three industries each provided

[4] "The Impact of Military Spending on the Machinists' Union," Marion Anderson Employment Research Associated (Lansing, Michigan, U.S.A.).

more than a million new jobs during the 1973–1979 period: "eating and drinking places," including fast food restaurants; "health services," including private hospitals, nursing homes, and doctors' and dentists' offices; and "business services," including personnel supply services, data processing services, reproduction and mailing and the quaintly named "services to buildings." These three industries together accounted for more than 40 percent of the new private jobs created between 1973 and the summer of 1980. In that period their employment increased almost three times as fast as total private employment, and sixteen times as fast as employment in the goods-producing or industrial sector of the economy.

The three "new" industries loom very large in total employment. Mr. Reagan's "fundamental manufacturing industries" are insignificant by comparison. Thus the increase in employment in eating and drinking places since 1973 is greater than total employment in the automobile and steel industries combined. Total employment in the three industries is greater than total employment in an entire range of basic productive industries; construction, all machinery, all electric and electronic equipment, motor vehicles, aircraft, ship building, all chemicals and products and all scientific and other instruments." [5]

Emma Rothschild sees in this a symptom of decay. These are low-wage activities giving little scope for technically progressive investments.

I do not see the force of this argument. If what the consumer most wants is to be freed from the chores of cooking and cleaning at home why is it less progressive to meet this demand than demand for objects made out of metals or chemicals? If they are low-wage occupations, the remedy is to unionise the workers and push up wages so that it would be profitable to mechanise the services, making fast food all the faster. This is certainly not a recipe for gracious living, but if it is what is wanted, why should it not be provided?

[5] Emma Rothschild, *Paradise Lost: The Decline of the Auto-Industrial Age* (New York: Random House, 1973).

The other two groups of services, concerned with health and finance, both require an increase is educated employment and should provide a large increase in professional jobs. How long will it take the economists in this country to see through the supply-side fallacy and return to a path of continuous growth?

Looking at the problem from a world point of view, W. W. Rostow, in your excellent *Economic Forum*, outlines a policy for supply-side development that makes sense. The threat to prosperity in the West comes essentially from the imbalance between demand and supply for energy. "The driving force in the sustained expansion the world economy requires in the 1980's should be enlarged investments in energy and energy conservation." [6]

But we have strayed too far into imagining what resources released from the arms race might be used for. Meanwhile the arms race is still going on and merely to point out that it is irrational will not stop it.

Professor Robert Neild in his forthcoming book *How to Make Up Your Mind About The Bomb* asks us, in a European setting, to estimate the unpleasantness of Russian hegemony (which he puts very high) and the likelihood of its being imposed in the absence of a nuclear deterrent (which he puts fairly low) and to decide in each country which has nuclear arms whether we consider that we have made a good bargain. But once we have got into this groove it is not easy to back out of it.

Alva Myrdal, who attended the Geneva discussions on SALT (Strategic Arms Limitation Talks) as the representative of Sweden, remarks upon the cost of *not* limiting arms:

> The arms race has brought costs to levels that are ruinous to the world economy. Even countries that are rich and technologically advanced are hampered in economic growth. After World War II, Germany, for a crucial period, and Japan until now were prohibited from spending their resources on arma-

[6] Vol. 11, no. 2, p. 30.

ments. This undoubtedly is part of the explanation why these countries had a growth rate that motivated analysts to speak of a miracle. Other developed countries in the postwar era would have shown a higher economic growth rate if they, too, had abstained from participating in the arms race; under-developed countries would have had a greater chance for development.

As the defense expenditures in the national budgets mount, it will become harder to obtain financing for the civilian purposes of health, education, housing and all other kinds of social needs. Public expenditures for such needs would, if well planned, increase productivity, as they are tantamount to investment in human capital which would raise the productivity of labour and prevent future remedial costs for individuals and society. In the long run, the arms race holds down civilian public expenditures, becoming thus an additional cause of stifling the rate of economic growth.

In underdeveloped countries, the allocation of scarce financial resources for the production or purchase of armaments will clearly have even more adverse effect than in the rich countries, having already hampered their economic development, grossly in some instances.

Military expenditure also plays a fateful role in the interrelations between richer and poorer nations. For example, there has been, globally speaking, a growing reluctance on the part of the richer, donor countries to give aid for development. One of the causes of this is the financial difficulties in the developed countries, and those are partly related to high expenditures for armaments.[7]

She gives a fascinating and horrifying account of how representatives on each side played into each other's hands to *prevent* a halt in the arms race which would cut down profits and employment in the arms industries.

Once a country is engulfed in the arms race, continuing it often appears as a means of preserving employment and the level of industrial production. Considered from the point of

[7] *The Game of Disarmament* (New York: Pantheon Books, 1976), pp. 8–9.

view of an individual armament-producing region of a country
or of a particular armament industry, this idea has a semblance
of truth, although arms production has been shown to represent relatively low demands for labour. To be sure, any realloca-
tion of resources always has initial difficulties and costs. These
should, however, not be over-estimated. They can be reduced if
conversion plans are outlined and established well in advance.

The arms race has become politically connected with the
vested interests that President Eisenhower termed "the military–industrial complex." In military matters, no limit is set
by market forces, by competitive demand or by prices. Every
new plant for military production, every new production contract, increases the weight of these vested interests. In democratic countries these interests, both labour and business, often
become rooted in the parliaments and the provincial assem-
blies, whose representatives are expected to defend local interests. In authoritarian countries, these vested interests should
be easier for a government to control, but apparently they are
not. [P. 10]

Moreover, there is an arms race within the arms race between
the three services — army, navy, and air force.

Industrial interests and imaginative scientists may have a
natural inclination for new inventions, but there are within the
military R&D establishments also strong bureaucratic pressures
to advance further. One reason for this is the interservice
competition for shares of the military budgets, leading to an
arms race within the arms race. This is difficult to control
"because of the sheer complexity and variety of modern specialized weapon systems," which complexity supports the military establishment in its opinion that only it is competent to
decide the size and character of the national security effort.
The situation is then "exploited to support claims for higher
military spending." If one service fears that its tasks are about
to be reduced, the pressures become considerable. [Pp. 11–12]

Robert Neild comments:

The SALT talks are an interesting example of inter-service
rivalry. All the rival military services are represented in the

negotiating teams of both sides and one can see that the agreements made so far have been so constructed that they do not oblige the two countries to make any marked change in the balance between strategic weapons operated by rival services. even though a change from vulnerable land-based missiles to submarine-launched missiles would make sense — and is permitted voluntarily. The representatives of the two superpowers from the armed services operating land-based missiles must have felt a common interest in avoiding obligatory reductions in that type of weapon. One wonders whether they, or their colleagues in other matching services, have ever explicitly acknowledged their common interest, in the conference chamber or outside it.[8]

Perhaps this complicity between the military, East and West, gives us a gleam of hope. Could they not agree to have a peace settlement *before* fighting a war? If they leave it till afterwards there will be nothing much left to settle.

---

[8] *How to Make Up Your Mind About the Bomb*, forthcoming.

THE TANNER LECTURERS

1976–77

Brasenose College, Oxford	Bernard Williams, Cambridge University
University of Michigan	Joel Feinberg, Brandeis University
Stanford University	Joel Feinberg, Brandeis University

1977–78

Brasenose College, Oxford	John Rawls, Harvard University
University of Michigan	Sir Karl Popper, University of London
Stanford University	Thomas Nagel, Princeton University

1978–79

Brasenose College, Oxford	Thomas Nagel, Princeton University
Clare Hall, Cambridge	C. C. O'Brien, London
University of Michigan	Edward O. Wilson, Harvard University
Stanford University	Amartya Sen, Oxford University
University of Utah	Lord Ashby, Cambridge University
Utah State University	R. M. Hare, Oxford University

1979–80

Brasenose College, Oxford	Jonathan Bennett, Syracuse University
Clare Hall, Cambridge	Raymond Aron, Collège de France
Harvard University	George J. Stigler, University of Chicago
University of Michigan	Robert Coles, Harvard University
Stanford University	Michel Foucault, Collège de France
University of Utah	Wallace Stegner, Los Altos Hills, California

1980–81

Brasenose College, Oxford	Saul Bellow, University of Chicago
Clare Hall, Cambridge	John Passmore, Australian National University
Harvard University	Brian Barry, University of Chicago
Hebrew University of Jerusalem	Solomon H. Snyder, Johns Hopkins University
University of Michigan	John Rawls, Harvard University
Stanford University	Charles Fried, Harvard University
University of Utah	Joan Robinson, Cambridge University

1981–82

Australian National University	Leszek Kolakowski, All Souls College, Oxford University; Yale University; University of Chicago
Brasenose College, Oxford	Freeman Dyson, Institute for Advanced Study, Princeton
Clare Hall, Cambridge	Kingman Brewster, New Haven, Connecticut
Harvard University	Murray Gell-Man, California Institute of Technology
University of Michigan	Thomas C. Schelling, Harvard University
Stanford University	Alan A. Stone, Harvard University
University of Utah	R. C. Lewontin, Harvard University

INDEX

ABM (Antiballistic missile) system, 72; abandonment of, 73, 75, 80

Air Force war plan (1951), 15–16

Alsop, Joseph, 100

Amundsen, Roald, 59, 61–63

Antiballistic missiles. *See* ABM system

"Armed peace," 83

Arms control: defined, 69–70; failures of, 79–81, 88–89; inspiration behind, 73, 82; military expenditures under, 79–88; responsibilities of, 81; ruling concept of U.S., 27; U.S. and Soviet agreements on, 71; vs. peace research, 87–88

Arms race, 25, 70, 72, 82–84, 94; as affected by SALT talks, 80; beginning of, 103–4; Cold War as cause of, 98–99, 110; cost of not limiting, 122–24; employment as motive for, 98, 119–20; inner momentum of, 106–7; interservice competition within, 124–25; momentum of research as cause of, 99–101, 103, 105, 110; power transferred to machines in, 108–9; and principle of effective demand, 110; role of scientific advisors in, 103–7

Army Field Manual FM-101-31-1, 17–20, 23–24

Assured Destruction, concept of, 27–31, 36–38, 41, 43; reasons to oppose, 28–30; vs. counterforce concept, 30–31; vs. facts, 27–28. *See also* Mutually Assured Destruction

Assured Survival concept, 43

Autism: as metaphor in nuclear struggle, 51–54

Balance of power: change in, 81–82; nuclear, 89

Balance of terror, 70, 107–8

Ballistic missile defense, 41

Bellow, Saul, 55

Blake, William, 50

Bohr, Niels, 101

Bradford, William, 48–51; *Of Plymouth Plantation*, 64

Brennan, Donald, "Brass Rule" principle of, 35–36

Brezhnev, Leonid, 72

British Bomber Command, 15

Brooke, Rupert, 7, 14

Brown, Harold (Secretary of Defense), 28

Brüning, Heinrich (Chancellor), 114–15

Caldicott, Helen, 94

Cambodia, 84, 87

Capitalism, theory on, as cause of war, 84–87

Capitalist world, center vs. periphery of, 85–87

Carter, Jimmy (President), 28, 79, 88

Carver, Field Marshall Lord, 23

Chemical and biological weapons, nonuse of, 71

Cherry-Garrard, Apsley, on heros, 59–62

Clausewitz, Karl von, maxim of, 80

Cold War as cause of arms race, 98–99, 103

Comedy, essential features of (essence of), 56, 58, 65

Counterforce: capability, 73–74, 76, 82; concept, 30–31, 43

Dallet, Joe, 8–10, 14, 23

Davy Crockett (warhead), 20–21

Descartes, 70

Detente, 90

Deterrence, 27, 107–8